NATIONAL
GEOGRAPHIC
KiDS

ULTIMATE
BOOK OF THE
FUTURE

INCREDIBLE, INGENIOUS, AND TOTALLY **REAL TECH**
THAT WILL CHANGE LIFE AS YOU KNOW IT

STEPHANIE WARREN DRIMMER

NATIONAL GEOGRAPHIC
WASHINGTON, D.C.

CONTENTS

CONTENTS

▲ In February 2021, NASA's Mars helicopter, named Ingenuity, landed on the red planet.

▶WELCOME TO THE FUTURE

FOR DECADES, people have dreamed of hoverboards, cities on Mars, and robots to do their bidding. Now, these technologies—and many more—might be closer than you think.

Today, we don't think twice about using a few clicks on a smartphone to text a friend, order a pizza, or buy a new outfit. But when your parents were kids, they didn't have cell phones. Go back another few generations, and there were no airplanes or even cars. Technologies that now power our everyday lives, like personal computers, GPS, and the internet, have all arrived in just the past few decades.

It might seem as if technology is accelerating, with new innovations being created at a faster and faster rate. That's because it actually is! Experts say that the more technology we get, the faster it improves. As we move into the future, new inventions will appear even more quickly than they do now.

All that means that we are living on the brink of a technology explosion. In your lifetime, you will experience more innovation than anyone else has in the history of time. Pretty cool, right?

No one can be sure what the future holds. (That's what makes it so exciting!) But within these pages, you'll find the best guesses from inventors, space experts, and brain scientists. Some of the technology they predict may never come to be. Other ideas are many years from becoming reality. But still other inventions and innovations are already in development. In fact, some of the technology in these pages, such as the Mars helicopter on page 64, went from a future possibility to a working machine in the time it took to write this book!

The future isn't some far-off fictional world. It's being shaped right now. To take a peek at what tomorrow might hold, just turn the page. Warning: If you've ever imagined zooming to school in a flying car or rocketing to a distant planet, then hang on tight. The future is one wild ride!

CHAPTER 1

THE FUTURE OF YOU

YOUR ALARM GOES OFF, WAKING YOU FROM A DEEP SLEEP. BUT THIS ALARM DOESN'T BLARE BEEP BEEP BEEP. INSTEAD, IT COAXES YOU OUT OF SLUMBER WITH THE ZESTY AROMA OF FRESHLY SQUEEZED ORANGE JUICE. ALL AROUND THE WORLD, INNOVATORS ARE CREATING DEVICES TO CHANGE YOUR EVERYDAY LIFE: EVERYTHING FROM CLOTHES THAT WASH THEMSELVES TO BIONIC BODY PARTS DESIGNED TO GIVE YOU SUPERPOWERS. READY TO SNEAK A PEEK AT YOUR LIFE IN THE FUTURE? READ ON!

ROBO-BUDDY

PERSONAL DROIDS

ON YOUR WAY HOME, you make a stop at the post office to pick up a package, then the grocery store to buy food for the week. Normally, all those purchases would be a lot to carry. But lucky for you, you have an assistant to do the toting for you: a personal droid.

In 2018, an Italian company called Piaggio introduced a new product: a droid made to carry heavy loads so people don't have to. Designed for city dwellers, Gita is meant to keep pedestrians' hands free, so they can chat on the phone or simply enjoy the walk without lugging bags. The droid pairs with a person, then follows him or her down the sidewalk, using cameras to see where it's going and gyroscopes to keep upright. The bot can carry up to 40 pounds (18 kg) and zip along at 22 miles an hour (35 km/h), fast enough to keep up with a person riding a bike.

Future personal droids might not even need a human to follow. Already, automated delivery bots are rolling down the sidewalks of cities like San Francisco, London, and Beijing. There, more and more people are relying on delivery services for their meals and supplies—but human couriers in trucks and cars are crowding the roads. Turning this task over to sidewalk-traveling bots might help clear traffic jams.

In the future, some experts think personal droids will be part of everyday life, not only delivering pizzas but also assisting gardeners, maintenance workers, people with disabilities, and anyone else who could use a helping hand.

+ FUN FACT
Famous science fiction droids include C-3PO and R2-D2 from *Star Wars*.

+ FUN FACT
Delivery robots have tons of tech to help them navigate crowded sidewalks: cameras, sensors, GPS navigation, and more.

◄ The Gita droid, developed by a company called Piaggio, was designed to follow its owner, carrying groceries and other items.

LOOK SMART
+ INTELLIGENT CLOTHING

IN THE FUTURE, getting dressed will be a snap. Our clothing won't just keep us covered; it will monitor the weather, give us directions, and even wash itself. Talk about a fashion statement!

+ WEATHER REPORT

Through a connection with your smartphone, this umbrella can alert you when it's going to rain and then—maybe even more usefully—let you know when you accidentally leave it behind.

+ OFF THE CUFF

What to do if you're on your bike—but you need to look up directions to your destination? This clothing looks like a normal jean jacket, but it has sensors built into the sleeve that allow cyclists to pause their music, answer a call, or check that next turn by just touching a cuff.

+ NICE AND TOASTY

When the U.S. Olympic team put on their uniforms in PyeongChang, South Korea, for the 2018 Winter Games, the temperatures were below freezing—but the athletes were nice and warm. Their parkas contained a special carbon-and-silver lining powered by a small battery pack to heat up the garment.

+ LAUNDRY NAY

Say goodbye to sweaty sports uniforms. Researchers are developing clothes covered with special microscopic structures to keep them clean. When exposed to light, the structures release a burst of energy that breaks down everything from soil to tomato sauce.

+ IT'S A SNAP

These contact lenses help the wearer take a picture in the blink of an eye—literally! They come with a built-in, microscopic camera that can be controlled by eye movements and blinking.

+ SHINE ON

Devices out of power? No problem—simply plug them into your outfit! A Dutch designer has already sent a line of sunlight-capturing clothes down the runway. Flexible solar panels collect energy when worn in direct sunlight, storing the power for charging smartphones and more.

THE FUTURE OF YOU

SUPER SUIT

EXOSKELETONS POWER UP

ON A CONSTRUCTION SITE, a worker lifts heavy building materials with ease. She grabs a bag of cement in one hand and tosses it like it weighs nothing. She stacks cinder blocks like they're children's building blocks. How is she managing these feats of strength? She's wearing a robotic suit that increases her strength by 20 times.

These robot suits are called industrial exoskeletons, and they're already in development. One named the Guardian XO uses sensors to monitor how the wearer moves her arms and legs. The suit mimics the speed, force, and direction of her motion and moves along with her, taking on most of the work. The makers say the suit makes carrying 100 pounds (45 kg) feel as light as five pounds (2.2 kg). In the future, some jobs may be taken over by robots, but others will still rely on humans. The Guardian XO is designed to help boost these workers' productivity and lessen injuries in construction sites and factories.

It's not the only super suit out there. Workers in car factories often have to hold their arms above their heads for long stretches of time as they work on the undersides of cars, which can cause injuries—and, of course, tired arms! Starting in 2018, workers in Ford car factories began wearing arm-supporting suits called EksoVests while on the job. Another exoskeleton, the Phoenix by suitX, is helping people who have been paralyzed walk again: Wearers push buttons in a pair of crutches to move the legs on command.

For now, these suits are expensive—the Phoenix costs around $40,000. But experts predict that the cost will drop in the future, and industrial exoskeletons will be everywhere. Companies are already working on new models to help the elderly get around and others to help athletes run longer distances without tiring. Talk about a power boost!

+ FUN FACT
The comic book character Iron Man gets extra strength and endurance from his high-tech exoskeleton.

▶ The Guardian XO exoskeleton was designed to make physically demanding work safer and easier for workers.

+ FUN FACT

Factory workers lift their arms as much as 4,600 times a day, or one million times a year.

▲ A man walks during physical therapy, with the help of the Phoenix exoskeleton.

GOING CYBORG

UPGRADING THE BODY

WHAT IF YOU COULD OUTRUN A RACEHORSE OR LEAP OVER A CAR? IN THE FUTURE, BODY ADD-ONS CALLED BIONICS MIGHT ALLOW US TO PUSH BEYOND THE LIMITS OF WHAT'S PHYSICALLY POSSIBLE. PEOPLE COULD UPGRADE THEIR NATURAL ABILITIES, TURNING FROM REGULAR HUMANS INTO REAL-LIFE SUPERHEROES.

▼BEYOND THE BODY

Erik Weihenmayer is a rock climber who regularly clings to sheer rock faces high off the ground. Weihenmayer is also blind. He climbs with a high-tech device that allows him to "see" the cliff he's scaling—with his tongue! Called the BrainPort, it looks like a video camera he wears on his forehead, attached to a white plastic lollipop he holds in his mouth. The camera converts the images it sees into electrical signals, which are then transmitted to the mouthpiece, buzzing the user's tongue in a pattern that represents what's in front of them. Over time, the brain can learn to interpret these signals to "see" the surroundings. (When he's not climbing, Weihenmayer can use the BrainPort to read.) In the future, users could don similar devices to sense all kinds of information, such as magnetic fields or the weather on another planet.

▲NEW DIRECTIONS

For most humans, setting off on a hike without a map, compass, or GPS device could be a recipe for disaster. But what if you could teach yourself to never be lost again? In 2014, a team of scientists in Germany outfitted test subjects with belts that vibrated whenever they were facing north—like a wearable compass. Over seven weeks, the subjects found the belt made it easier for them to find their way, helping them know which direction to face when leaving an underground train station, for example. This kind of wearable bionic could help future humans upgrade their brains with superior navigation knowledge.

B6 (128mm × 182mm)

A5 (148mm × 210mm)

Dolphins, bats, and whales can also "see" in the dark—using a sense called echolocation. They send out blips of sound, which bounce off objects and travel back to the animal's ears. By listening to these echoes, the animals can detect where objects are and even tell their size and shape. Recently, a group of inventors has been working to give humans the same sense. Their device, called the Bottlenose, uses high-pitched sound to locate objects in a dark room, then sends the echoes to vibrate sensors worn on the user's skin. The closer the user moves to an object, the stronger the signal.

▶ **SUPER VISION**

Some snakes can hunt in complete darkness, pinpointing the exact location of a mouse and striking with deadly precision. To do it, they use a special sense that allows them to "see" in the dark. Organs in their faces can detect infrared radiation—a type of energy invisible to humans. But someday, we might be able to sense it just like snakes can. In 2019, scientists at the University of Science and Technology of China injected mice with tiny particles that stuck to the light-detecting cells in their eyes, allowing the mice to see infrared light. It's far too early to use the technology on humans—but someday it could allow us to see in the dark.

BUGS FOR BREAKFAST

THE FUTURE OF FOOD

TIME FOR BREAKFAST! You pour your favorite cereal into a bowl and grab a spoon. But there's something a little different about these future flakes—they're made of ground-up crickets and mealworms! That might sound odd to some, but in many cultures, bugs are a common addition to the menu. And many experts believe that in the future, people all over the world will be munching on insects.

Every year, the planet's population grows by 70 million. By 2050, we'll need 70 percent more food than is currently produced on Earth to feed all those hungry mouths. But we're already running low on space for farming. We need to figure out a type of food that makes better use of the space we already have. And many experts think insects are the answer.

Insects are rich in proteins, vitamins, and minerals. They don't need nearly as much room as cows or chickens—in fact, they thrive in dark, crowded conditions. They need little water. And perhaps most important, bugs give a lot of bang for your buck: For every two pounds (0.9 kg) of feed, a farmer can get 12 times more edible protein from crickets than he could from beef.

That might not be enough to convince you to replace your grub with, well, grubs. But two

billion people around the world already eat insects. In Thailand, people snack on grasshoppers, crickets, and woodworms that have been fried until crispy. In Ghana, people munch on termites in the springtime when other food is scarce. To help convince skeptics, some companies are already turning crickets into flour that can be made into snack chips, protein bars, and smoothie powders—no crunchy legs involved!

+ FUN FACT

Termites have a minty flavor.

+ FUN FACT

Lobsters, crabs, and other shellfish are closely related to insects.

[COULD IT HAPPEN?]

▶ COULD A ROBOT BECOME PRESIDENT?

ARTIFICIAL INTELLIGENCE (AI) is beginning to take on all kinds of jobs that were once only for humans. There are computer systems that can diagnose diseases, research legal cases, and even write songs. AI can do many of the tasks people can—and sometimes do them better. So is it possible that someday, we might have a robot do one of the most important jobs of all: leading a nation?

MIND THE MACHINE

The idea might sound far-fetched. But in 2016, one group pushed for Watson, the *Jeopardy!*-winning AI developed by IBM, to run for president of the United States. They thought a bot could make a good leader because unlike humans, robots never make decisions based on emotion. While humans can be influenced by anger, prejudice, and ego, robots would in theory use only the facts when choosing a course of action.

People who support voting for a robot also argue that computers are better than humans at processing huge amounts of information. A human president can't keep up with every detail coming in from government agencies, the economy, the people, the press, and more. But artificial intelligence can. To answer each *Jeopardy!* question, Watson instantly analyzed 200 million pages of information—including all of Wikipedia. A future robot president could go further, basing every decision on all of human knowledge. To boot, a robot would work harder than any human in history, never stopping to sleep or get a snack.

BRAINY BOT?

Even most people in favor of a robo-president say our current AI isn't ready yet. Our most advanced programs, such as Watson, can only do one task. A robot ruler would need to solve many kinds of different problems, from how to negotiate with other countries to how to handle the changing climate.

Another hurdle is that computers aren't great communicators. They can process massive amounts of information to make a decision—but they can't explain their thought process afterward. While a human president can talk through why they did what they did and explain their actions to the people, a computer might leave the country in the dark. And, as for prejudice, AI is currently only as unbiased as its programming. Some AI has shown trouble distinguishing between light-skinned and dark-skinned people, or people of different genders. Some experts say AI will never measure up. Others think it will overcome these obstacles within the next few decades.

Would you vote for a robot?

▲ The "face" of Watson, an advanced computer system that faced off against human competitors on the game show *Jeopardy!*

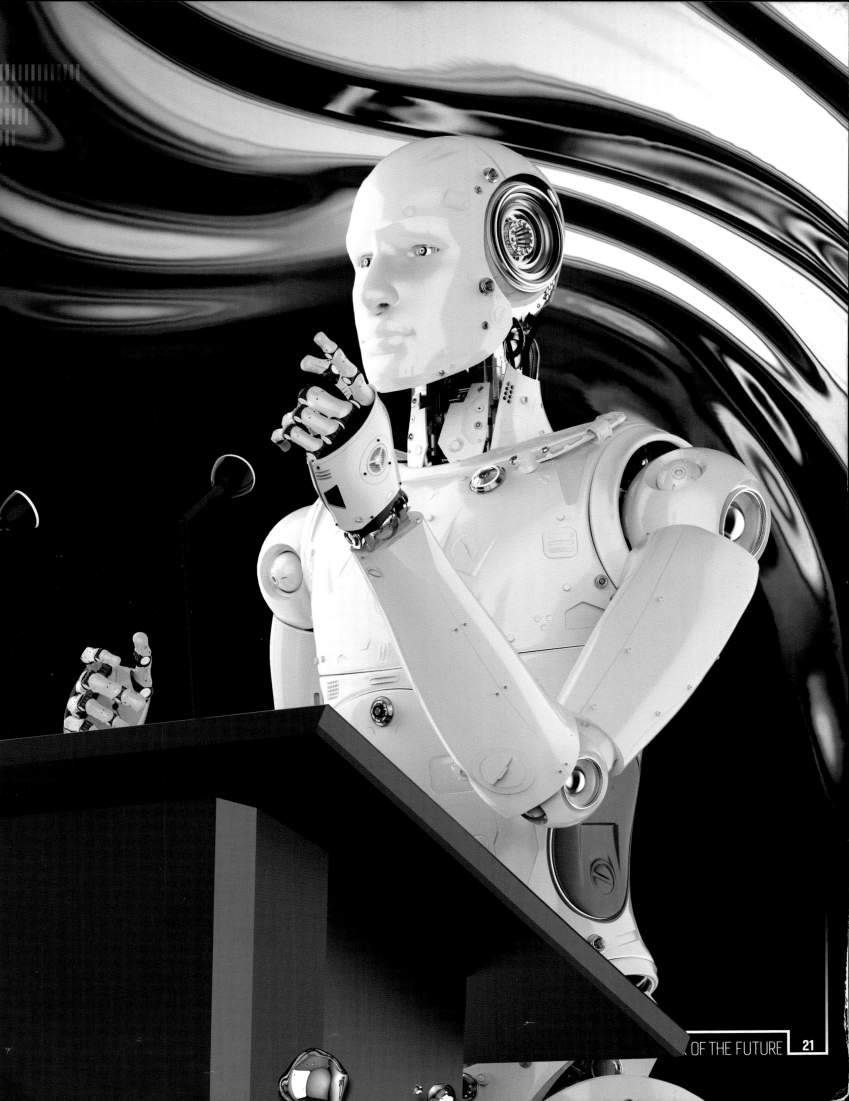

THEN VS. NOW

▶ MEAL IN A PILL

THEN ▼

ON FEBRUARY 20, 1962, astronaut John Glenn quenched his thirst by sipping an orange-flavored drink from a pouch. The drink, called Tang, was made from a powdered mix of sugar, coloring, and vitamins C and A. From then on, people assumed, it was only a matter of time before this high-tech space food became food for Earthlings, too. Soon, we'd be getting all our daily nutrients simply by swallowing a pill. No more time wasted cooking, eating, and cleaning up!

NOW ▼

TANG HAD BEEN SITTING ON GROCERY STORE SHELVES, mostly untouched, for years before its ride through space. It wasn't until John Glenn drank the orange liquid as he orbited Earth at 17,000 miles an hour (27,000 km/h) that Tang took off on Earth, too. Many people (falsely) believed it had been developed by NASA, and American shoppers slurped up what seemed like the food of the future. Hungry for even more instant foods, they started buying up nondairy creamer, dehydrated soups, and instant mashed potatoes.

But what about something even more instant than instant food? Since the end of the 19th century, futurists had predicted that technology would allow us to condense our meals down to their essentials, extract the exact mix of nutrients needed to keep us alive and healthy, and put them in pill form. Fast-forward to the present, and we're still sitting down three times a day for meals. Why?

The problem is that there's no way to fit the calories a human needs to survive into a pill. An average adult human has to eat about 2,250 calories each day. (Calories measure the amount of energy that food contains.) Even with the highest-calorie foods, like butter and oil, you'd need more than a cup to hit your minimum. Add other essentials, like fiber, and you've got a pill that's far too big to swallow.

◄ In 1962, astronaut John Glenn became the first American to eat in space.

CHANGING SPACES

A TRANSFORMING HOME

IT'S THE YEAR 2040. You get home from work and open the door to your apartment. It has all the comforts you could hope for: A guest bedroom, a full-size kitchen—even a home theater and a gym! And that all fits inside about 300 square feet—the size of many peoples' living room. How is this possible?

The secret is a transformable home: One that can change depending on the needs of the person who lives there. In a concept transformable home built by the LAAB architect firm, the bathtub gets a special cover topped with cushions that change it into a sofa. If a guest visits, it can transform again into a screened guest bedroom. In the kitchen, the ceiling opens to reveal cabinets, and the floor opens for extra storage.

This concept isn't just for fun. City living is cramped, and in the future, space is about to get even tighter. At the beginning of the 20th century, there were one billion people living on Earth. By 2037, experts estimate the world population will hit nine billion. And by 2050, two-thirds of those people will be living in cities. They're going to need smart space solutions.

Other concept transformable homes have beds that hoist up to the ceiling when not in use, dining tables that sink down seamlessly into the floor, and even a kitchen that folds down to space-saving size. Now that's a smart home!

+ FUN FACT

In the future, your bed could vanish into the ceiling when you're not sleeping in it!

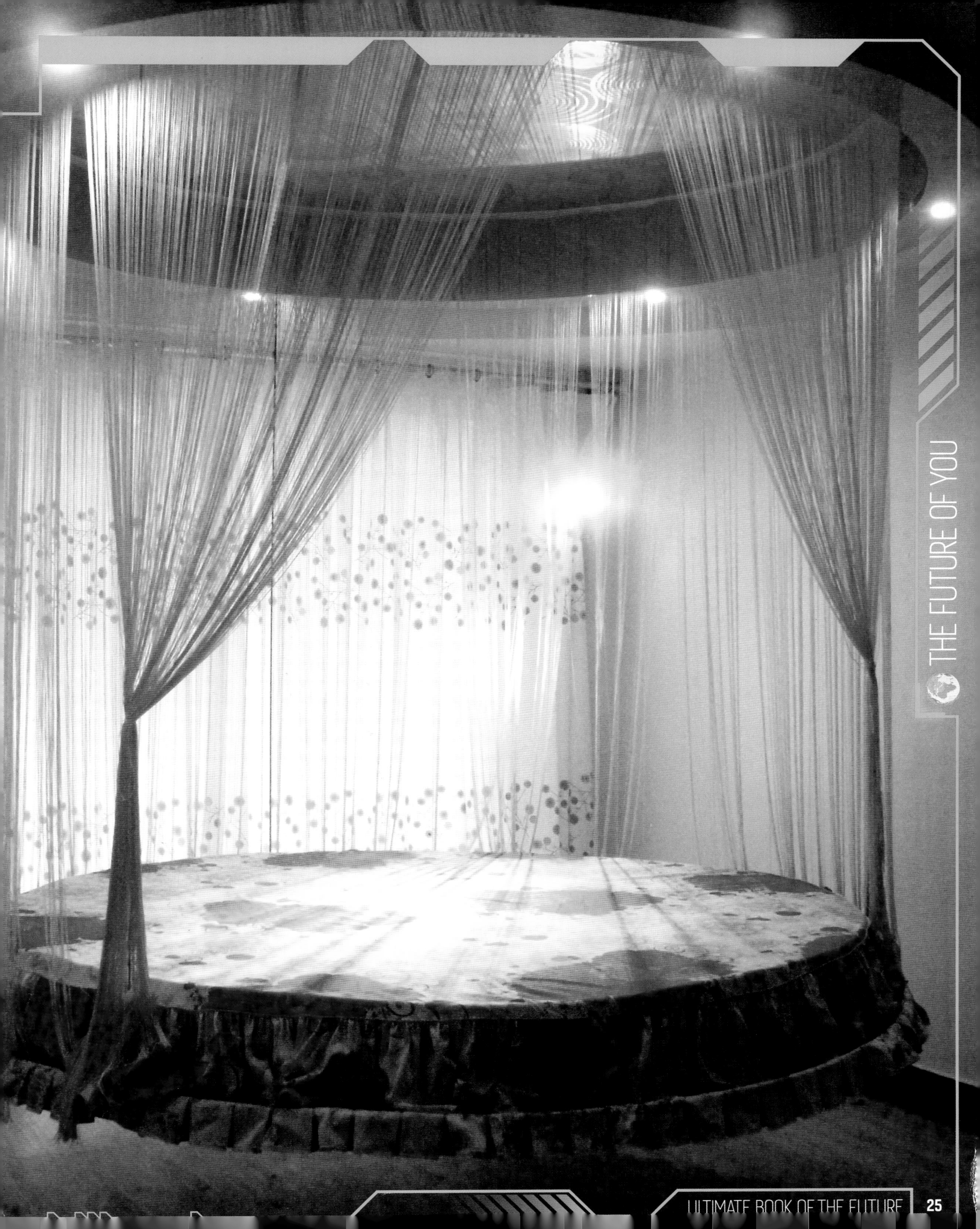

FUTURE PETS

FROM WOOF TO BEEP

AT LEAST 10,000 YEARS AGO, ANCIENT HUMANS AND WILD WOLVES FORMED A FAST FRIENDSHIP. OVER TIME, THE WOLVES BECAME FRIENDLY. THEIR EARS TURNED FLOPPY AND THEIR TEETH SHRANK. DOGS WERE THE FIRST DOMESTICATED ANIMALS; NEXT CAME CATS. HUMANS HAVE HAD PETS FOR THOUSANDS OF YEARS, AND WE'LL LIKELY CONTINUE TO FOR THOUSANDS MORE. BUT WHAT WILL THOSE FUTURE FURRY FRIENDS LOOK LIKE?

▶ ROBO-PETS

Cuddling with a fluffy friend—awesome. Scooping poop—not so much. But in the future, pets might be mess free. Engineers are designing robots that will move like real-live animals, able to chase a ball or jump in your lap. Tombot is a furry bot that looks like a puppy, wags its tail, barks on command, and leans in for a scratch behind the ears. Tombot and other robotic pets have been shown to lower levels of depression and agitation in dementia patients—just like real pets, but without the walks, food, or vet visits.

◀ FLUORESCENT FIDO

Would you want a dog with a solid coat? A spotted one? What about a coat that glows? Since 2003, genetically engineered aquarium fish called GloFish have been for sale in pet stores. Scientists inserted DNA from naturally fluorescent jellyfish into the fish's DNA, creating critters that light up in fluorescent rainbow colors. In 2009, scientists used the same technique to create the world's first glowing dogs: four beagle puppies that shine red under ultraviolet light. The pups were for scientific research, but someday the technology could be used to create light-up pets.

▶ PET ENTERTAINMENT

What do Fluffy and Fido do all day while their pet parents are at work and school? In the future, owners will turn to technology to keep their pets happy and entertained when they're home alone. Already, a device called iCPooch lets people check in with their dogs—and even videochat with them—during the day. Another, called Kittyo, allows owners to touch a finger to their phone screen to move a laser dot around the room at home for their cat's entertainment.

▲ DINOSAUR CHICKENS

Many people keep backyard chickens. Someday, they could keep backyard dinosaurs. That might sound far-out, but birds actually are dinosaurs: They're descended from the same dino group that included velociraptors and *T. rex.* Now, a paleontologist named Jack Horner is attempting to make genetic tweaks to chickens to give them characteristics of their Jurassic ancestors, including clawed arms, teeth, and long tails.

▼ SPEAKING DOG

Have you ever wondered what your dog was thinking? Soon, you might know for sure. At North Carolina State University, U.S.A., a group of researchers are developing a "smart harness" that will help humans connect to their canines. The harness has sensors that monitor the dog's heart rate and other body responses. In the future, it could send owners a text message letting them know when their pet is stressed or relaxed.

FUTURE PHONES

A GENIE IN YOUR POCKET

IMAGINE UNFOLDING YOUR PHONE until it's the size of a computer screen. Instead of touching it with your fingers, you use eye movements to pull up an image, edit it, and send it to a friend. Meanwhile, your phone is charging without needing to be plugged in. These advancements might sound far off, but they could all be part of your future smartphone.

OLD TECH

Already, our phones don't just make calls. They are powerful computers that remind us of appointments, store our family photos, connect us to social networks, and entertain us with games and videos. They're so advanced that a single modern smartphone has thousands of times more computer power than the computers that took humans to the moon!

All that advancement has happened quickly. Cell phones didn't even exist until 1973, when an engineer named Martin Cooper became the first person to make a call on a portable mobile device. It weighed more than two pounds (0.9 kg), took 10 hours to charge enough for a 35-minute chat, and cost $3,995. Phones have come far since then—so what will the future hold?

▲ Martin Cooper poses with a hefty early cell phone.

13:13

G

Galaxy Store　　นาฬิกา　　ปฏิ

NEW LOOK

In the late 1990s and early 2000s, flip phones were everywhere. These clamshell-style devices folded shut after the user completed the call or text. Now, flip phones are coming back, but in a different way. Many companies are experimenting with a new style of phones with screens made of plastic, not glass, that can fold out to the size of a tablet when the user needs a bigger screen to work with.

New cameras will change the look of future phones, too. Designs with as many as nine lenses on the back could boost the power of onboard cameras by shooting multiple pics simultaneously, then digitally stitching them together into one large photo. Using multiple lenses could also help users zoom better and create photos with artfully blurred backgrounds, just like high-tech professional cameras.

CALLING ON THE FUTURE

Future phones won't just look different; they'll work differently, too. Since short battery life is the main complaint people have with their current phones, companies are working on ways to charge smarter. Prototype phones can now recharge from low-level power in the form of radio frequencies or infrared light beamed through the air. Experts say transmitters that emit this energy could be placed in household objects such as lightbulbs so that your phone will charge right in your pocket as you go about your day.

After that, what's next? Someday, your phone might disappear entirely. Smart glasses that connect with a phone can already track users' head movements and hand gestures. In the future, experts predict, the glasses will be powerful enough that they don't need to be paired with a phone. Now that's something to talk about!

THE FUTURE OF YOU

+ FUN FACT
There are more mobile devices than there are people in the world.

FUTURE FAIL

HYGIENE MACHINE ▼

MORE THAN 50 YEARS AGO, the futuristic TV family the Jetsons blasted into living rooms across America. They showed off a vision for a world full of flying cars, holograms, and aliens. Thanks to their technology of tomorrow, every aspect of the Jetsons' lives was faster and easier—starting from the moment they woke up in the morning. After they rolled out of bed, the Jetsons would simply press a button and a long arm would emerge from the wall, whip a toothbrush around, and clean their teeth in seconds. Now, we're living in the future the Jetsons promised. So where are our automatic toothbrushes?

Of course, we do have toothbrushes that do some of the work for us: The first electric toothbrush, called the Broxodent, was invented in Switzerland in 1954. It plugged into the wall, but it was soon followed by a cordless version, the General Electric Automatic Toothbrush, in the early 1960s. Despite its name, it was nowhere near automatic. Today, we're still not there: Not only are we missing out on a robot to clean our teeth without effort, we still have to style our own hair and put on our clothes ourselves.

▲ The Jetsons enjoy a whole suite of automated luxuries.

FAIL

◄ Electric toothbrushes vibrate on their own, but they still, sadly, need a human to maneuver them.

CHAPTER 2
GETTING AROUND

OH NO! YOU'RE LATE FOR SCHOOL! GOOD THING IT'S THE FUTURE, AN AGE OF JETPACKS, PASSENGER DRONES ... AND MAYBE EVEN TELEPORTATION. YOU HOP ABOARD YOUR VEHICLE OF CHOICE AND ZOOM AWAY IN TIME TO MAKE IT BEFORE THE BELL RINGS.

TODAY, INVENTORS AND SCIENTISTS ALL OVER THE WORLD ARE BUSY DREAMING UP NEW WAYS TO GET US FROM PLACE TO PLACE FASTER THAN EVER BEFORE. ARE YOU READY FOR THE RIDE OF A LIFETIME?

TAKING FLIGHT

PERSONAL JETPACKS

ON MAY 10, 2011, a yellow dot appeared in the air above the Grand Canyon. It was Yves "the Jetman" Rossy, a Swiss pilot and the inventor of an experimental jetpack, testing out his creation. Rossy dropped from a helicopter and soared 200 feet (61 m) over the rim of the canyon, hitting speeds of 190 miles an hour (306 km/h) before parachuting down to the base. The flight lasted eight minutes.

People have been trying to build a practical jetpack since the 1960s, when films showed heroes like James Bond zooming through the air on rocket power. But their early attempts used very expensive substances for fuel and burned through them fast. They were also extremely difficult to pilot, and more than one brave stuntman was injured in flight.

Then, in the 2010s, jetpacks started zipping onto the scene again. Some were held aloft by jets of water. Others, like Rossy's, were gas-powered, but they couldn't take off from or land on the ground: They had to be dropped from the sky by another aircraft. These weren't the true jetpacks promised by the movies.

But that kind of jetpack might finally be on the horizon. In 2017, British inventor Richard Browning unveiled the Gravity jet suit—with jets on the pilot's forearms and back. In 2018, Grand Canyon flier Rossy released a documentary teaser that shows him launching from the ground via his winged version for the first time. And a company called JetPack Aviation has become the first to sell a jetpack to consumers: It can whiz by at up to 120 miles an hour (193 km/h) and fly for 10 minutes. All it takes is $340,000, and, of course, a pilot brave enough to get airborne.

▲ Yves Rossy jets above the Grand Canyon.

+ FUN FACT

In 2019, JetPack Aviation introduced a jet-powered flying motorcycle called the Speeder.

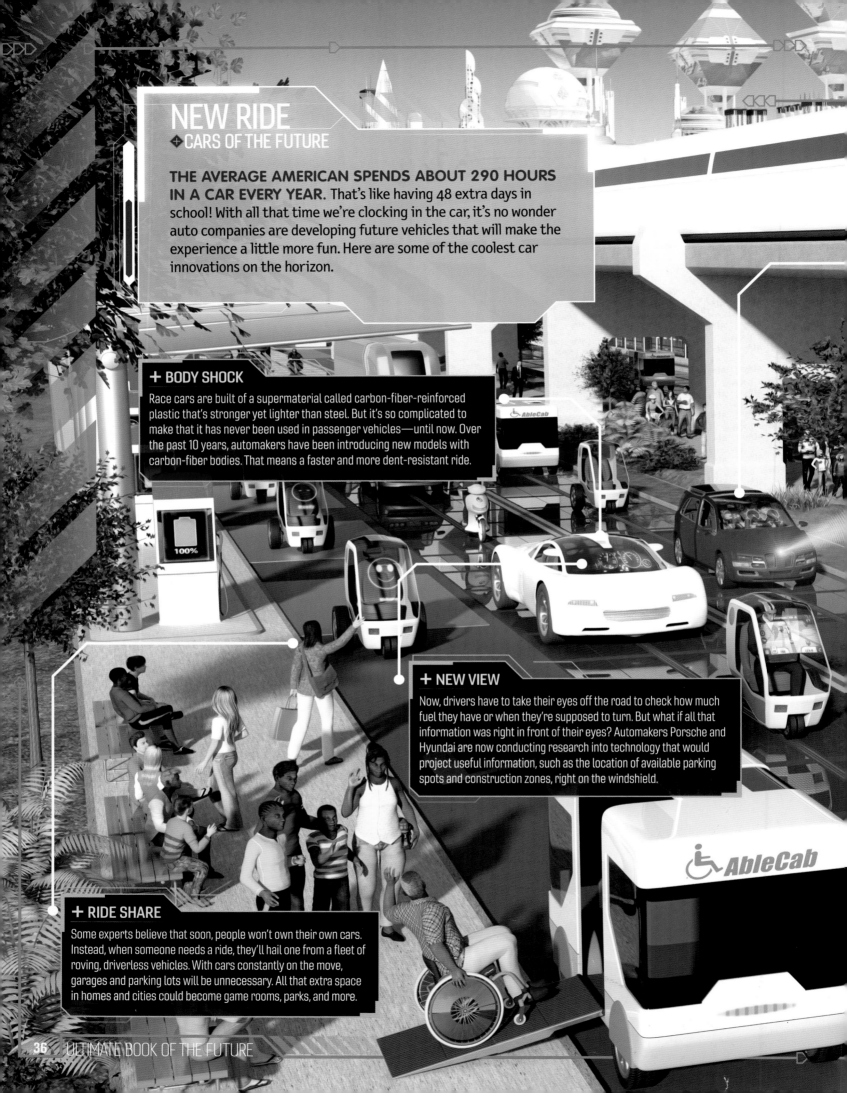

NEW RIDE
✛ CARS OF THE FUTURE

THE AVERAGE AMERICAN SPENDS ABOUT 290 HOURS IN A CAR EVERY YEAR. That's like having 48 extra days in school! With all that time we're clocking in the car, it's no wonder auto companies are developing future vehicles that will make the experience a little more fun. Here are some of the coolest car innovations on the horizon.

+ BODY SHOCK

Race cars are built of a supermaterial called carbon-fiber-reinforced plastic that's stronger yet lighter than steel. But it's so complicated to make that it has never been used in passenger vehicles—until now. Over the past 10 years, automakers have been introducing new models with carbon-fiber bodies. That means a faster and more dent-resistant ride.

+ NEW VIEW

Now, drivers have to take their eyes off the road to check how much fuel they have or when they're supposed to turn. But what if all that information was right in front of their eyes? Automakers Porsche and Hyundai are now conducting research into technology that would project useful information, such as the location of available parking spots and construction zones, right on the windshield.

+ RIDE SHARE

Some experts believe that soon, people won't own their own cars. Instead, when someone needs a ride, they'll hail one from a fleet of roving, driverless vehicles. With cars constantly on the move, garages and parking lots will be unnecessary. All that extra space in homes and cities could become game rooms, parks, and more.

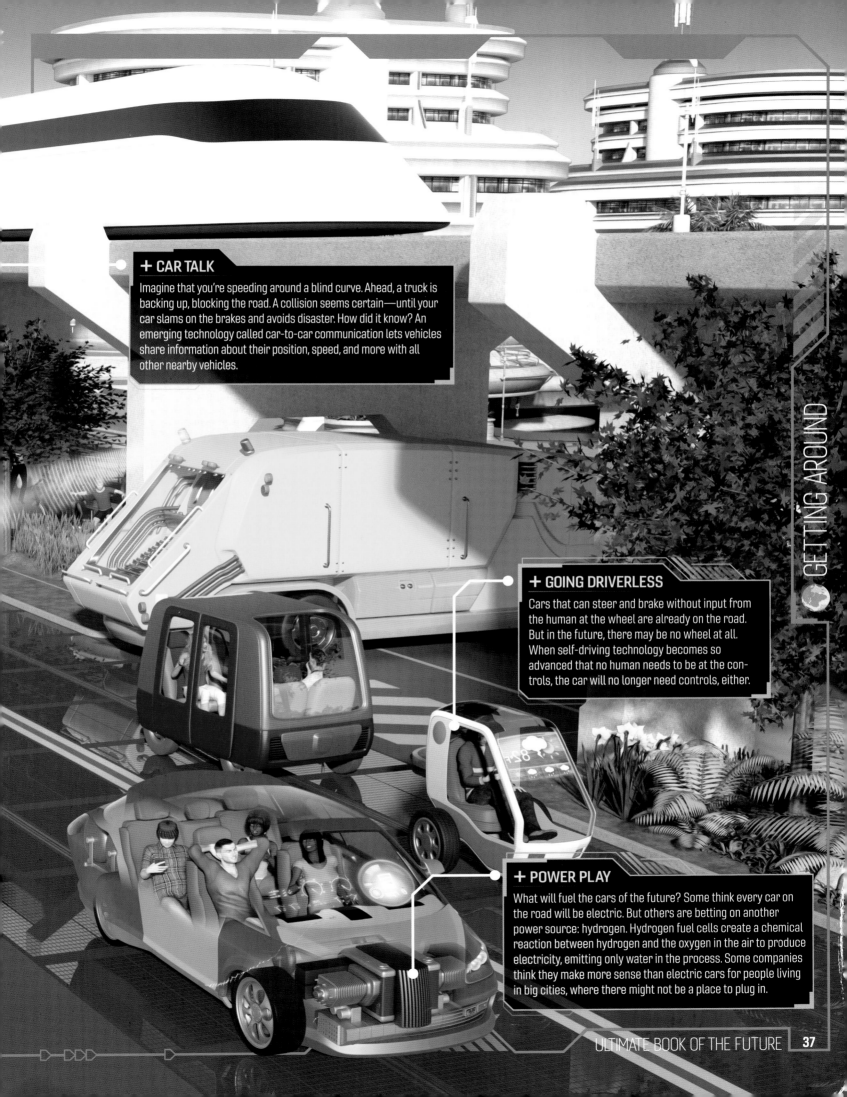

+ CAR TALK

Imagine that you're speeding around a blind curve. Ahead, a truck is backing up, blocking the road. A collision seems certain—until your car slams on the brakes and avoids disaster. How did it know? An emerging technology called car-to-car communication lets vehicles share information about their position, speed, and more with all other nearby vehicles.

+ GOING DRIVERLESS

Cars that can steer and brake without input from the human at the wheel are already on the road. But in the future, there may be no wheel at all. When self-driving technology becomes so advanced that no human needs to be at the controls, the car will no longer need controls, either.

+ POWER PLAY

What will fuel the cars of the future? Some think every car on the road will be electric. But others are betting on another power source: hydrogen. Hydrogen fuel cells create a chemical reaction between hydrogen and the oxygen in the air to produce electricity, emitting only water in the process. Some companies think they make more sense than electric cars for people living in big cities, where there might not be a place to plug in.

THEN VS. NOW

►FLYING CARS

►Glenn Curtiss made many contributions to plane and motorcycle technology.

THEN ▼

IN 1911, an inventor named Glenn Curtiss debuted the Autoplane, a three-seater, car-shaped vehicle outfitted with wings on the top and propellers on the back and front. It was only a matter of time, spectators figured, before everybody was whizzing around above the ground to school and work. But the prototype failed to impress on its maiden voyage: It managed nothing more than a few short hops. More than a century later, we're still waiting on our flying cars.

▲ Lilium, a German aviation company, has been designing flying vehicles since 2015—starting with a two-seater prototype and evolving into five-seater and seven-seater models.

ALL THAT WAITING MAY FINALLY BE COMING TO AN END. Some futurists think we're now on the cusp of having flying cars. Today, dozens of companies have air transit vehicles in development, and many already have working prototypes.

There's the Jet, a flying vehicle invented by German company Lilium. Electrically powered engines mounted on its wing flaps allow it to take off by rising vertically into the air, then fly horizontally like a normal airplane. Lilium envisions Jets stationed in major cities, able to whisk passengers from place to place much faster than taxis or trains. The company predicts a flight between Manhattan, New York, and John F. Kennedy International Airport will take six minutes, a trip that now takes at least an hour.

Ride-hailing company Uber is serious about taking its service to the skies: Uber promised to put a fleet of flying taxi drones into the air in the 2020s. (Experts are skeptical.) Uber has since handed the program off to a company called Joby Aviation, but the taxis are still in the works. Like the Jet, the vehicle will be electrically powered and designed to take off and land vertically, meaning there's no runway needed. Air taxi services may partner with real estate companies to develop "sky ports" where people can catch a ride in cities around the United States. Maybe this time, the flying car might truly be about to take off.

▲ The Autoplane was an early attempt at a flying car.

ALL ABOARD

TRAINS OF TOMORROW

THE WORLD'S FIRST RAILWAY PASSENGERS climbed aboard a steam locomotive in September 1825 for a bone-shaking ride. Most of the 300 travelers stood in open wagons, some sitting on top of sacks of coal and flour. It wasn't what you'd call a wild ride: The train traveled 8.5 miles (14 km) in two hours, reaching a top speed of 15 miles an hour (24 km/h) across northeast England. Trains are the oldest form of mass transportation, and today, it seems like some railways are still stuck in the 1800s. But trains are about to get a whole new top speed.

FLOATING TRAINS

On October 19, 2016, a Japanese train broke records when it hit a dizzying 375 miles an hour (603 km/h), covering nearly 20 football fields in less than 11 seconds. (Meanwhile, the United States' "high-speed" train, run by Amtrak, tops out at 150 miles an hour [241 km/h].)

The record-breaking train runs on technology called maglev, short for magnetic levitation. Maglev trains have no wheels. Instead, they have a set of special, superpowered magnets. These magnets repel against another set of magnets in the track, lifting the train so it hovers ever so slightly. Then, another set of magnets pushes the train forward along the track. By floating the train above the track, maglev cancels out the slowing force of friction, making it possible for its trains to travel many times faster than traditional ones.

There are already a few maglev train systems operating around the world today, and many countries have plans to open more in the future. Japan's Chuo Shinkansen line promises to take passengers between Tokyo and Osaka, a distance of 247 miles (397 km), in less than an hour.

▲ The Hyperloop would send passenger trains through tubes at superfast speeds.

LOOP THE LOOP

The other major type of futuristic train isn't really a train at all. Called Hyperloop, it's the brainchild of U.S. entrepreneur Elon Musk, who dreamed of a system that can carry people between San Francisco and Los Angeles, a distance of 380 miles (611 km), in less than half an hour—faster than an airplane.

While a maglev train eliminates the friction between a train's wheels and the track, the train is still slowed by friction from the air it travels through. Musk's idea is to eliminate friction almost completely. Passenger-carrying pods would speed through tunnels that have had most of their air removed, reducing friction. To lower friction even more, the pods would be held above the ground by a layer of air, similar to how the puck floats above the table in a game of air hockey. Musk predicts the Hyperloop's pods will be able to travel at 670 miles an hour (1,078 km/h).

Today, teams around the world are competing to make the Hyperloop a reality. In 2018, a team of German engineering students developed a small-scale prototype that reached speeds of 284 miles an hour (457 km/h). The system is far from ready for passengers. But someday, it could transform travel.

+ FUN FACT

Trains in Copenhagen, Denmark, operate without drivers.

+ FUN FACT

Japan's bullet train lines have networks of in-ground sensors that activate emergency brakes if they detect an earthquake.

► COULD HUMANS TELEPORT?

HAVE YOU EVER WONDERED WHAT IT WOULD BE LIKE if you could instantly transport yourself from one place to another? Instead of circling the same old neighborhood, you could walk the streets of Shanghai, China. Instead of eating the same old takeout for dinner, you could dine in Paris, France. You could even visit the moon or the rings of Saturn. Science fiction characters have been using teleportation to get around for decades. But of course, that's just made up ... or is it?

STARTING SMALL

Teleportation is very real. But it's not the kind that appears in science fiction. Real-life teleportation uses the principles of quantum physics, a set of rules that describe the strange behavior of photons, electrons, and other minuscule particles that make up the universe. In the quantum world, the regular rules of the universe don't apply: Bits of matter can bop in and out of existence. Particles act sometimes like solid clumps and other times like waves.

One of the strangest phenomena in the quantum world is called quantum entanglement. When two particles are "entangled," it doesn't mean that they're twisted around one another. Instead, it means that the actions of one affect the actions of the other. In the lab, scientists have learned how to entangle two particles, then deliberately change one of them. When they do, the other particle will instantly change, too—even if the two particles are far apart. In 2017, Chinese scientists used this principle to "teleport" information from one particle on Earth to another on a satellite in space.

▼ Characters in *Star Trek* use a transporter to teleport to and from their ship.

THINKING BIG

The Chinese experiment might seem nothing like teleportation. But consider this: It means information was transmitted faster than the speed of light, thought to be the speed limit of the universe. In quantum teleportation, a bit of information goes from one particle to another without physically passing between them. It moves in an instant, without traveling.

Of course, there's a big difference between sending a chunk of information hopping from one spot to another and sending a human being. In theory, it could be possible to analyze the state of every atom in a person's body and transmit it to a new location, where the person could be reassembled atom by atom. But the human body contains around seven billion billion billion atoms. We have nowhere near the processing power to handle all that data. Yet some scientists believe that there is nothing in the laws of physics that says human teleportation is impossible. Maybe we just have to wait for the future to unlock this transportation riddle.

Where would you go if you could teleport?

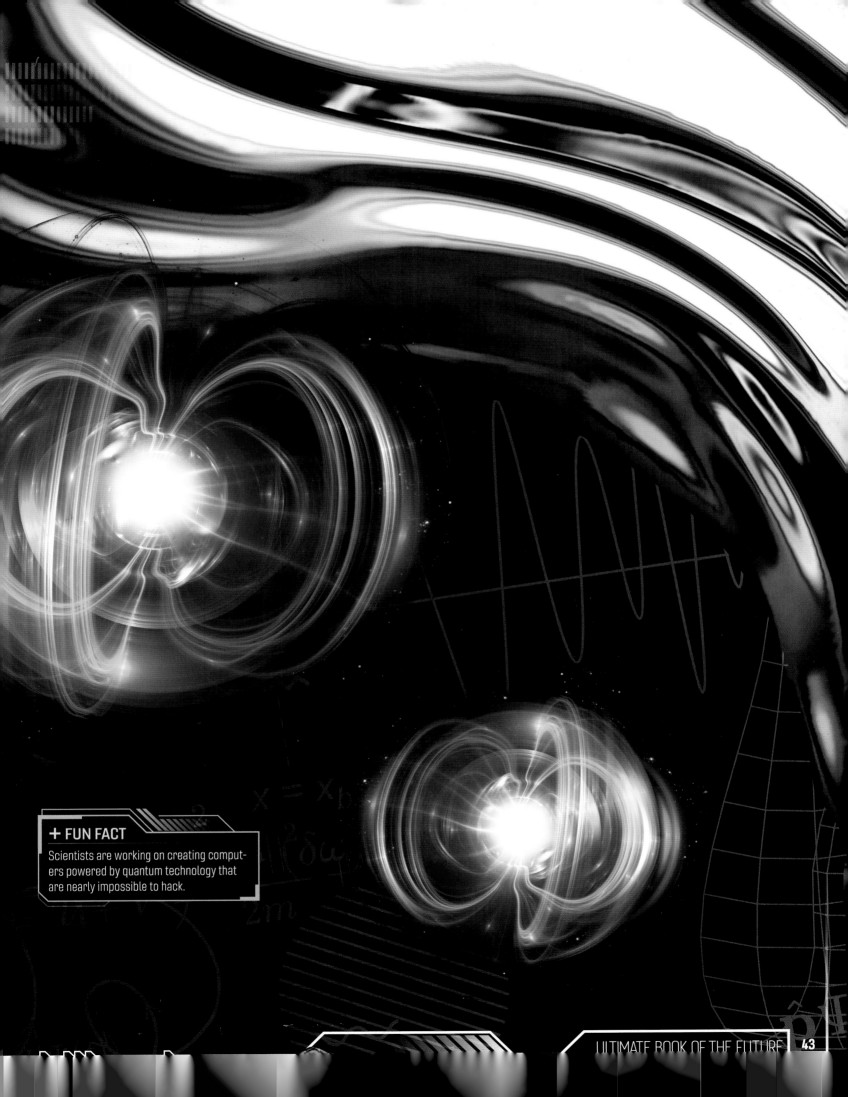

+ FUN FACT

Scientists are working on creating computers powered by quantum technology that are nearly impossible to hack.

OCEAN EXPLORER

UNDERWATER TRANSFORMER

A BRIGHT ORANGE SUBMARINE floats through the water. Then, it begins to change. Its top rises up, and from within the machine, two limbs emerge and unfold. They're robot arms, equipped with claw-like grippers: This is Aquanaut, a real-life Transformer that can glide through the sea in underwater vehicle mode, then switch into two-armed explorer mode to do work under the waves.

Aquanaut is the brainchild of engineers at Houston Mechatronics Inc., in Texas. They hoped to create a machine that could travel like a submarine to an underwater destination, then transform into a humanoid form capable of using tools. The bot can perform tasks such as fixing broken parts on a deep-sea well. All the while, a human team communicates with Aquanaut from the safety of the shore.

Some places—like the deepest parts of the ocean—are tough for humans to travel to. Lack of light, extreme cold, and crushing pressure put people in danger. That's why many experts say that high-tech robots like Aquanaut are the future of exploration. Instead of putting themselves in harm's way, people can send robots equipped with cameras and sensors in their place.

In the future, bots like Aquanaut may travel even farther than the deep ocean. A NASA project called the Systematic Underwater Biogeochemical Science and Exploration Analog, or SUBSEA, is currently testing underwater robots to explore deep-sea volcanoes off the coast of Hawaii. They believe the conditions there are similar to those of Saturn's moon Enceladus, an icy world covered with geysers that shoot water out from its below-surface ocean. Someday, bots like Aquanaut could travel to Enceladus in place of human astronauts, to find out what—or who—lurks there.

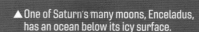

▲ One of Saturn's many moons, Enceladus, has an ocean below its icy surface.

+ FUN FACT

Aquanauts and astronauts alike train in NASA's Neutral Buoyancy Laboratory, a giant swimming pool that mimics the weightlessness of space.

+ FUN FACT

In 2019, a submersible ROV (remotely operated vehicle) caught video footage of a living giant squid for only the second time in history.

DRONE DRIVER

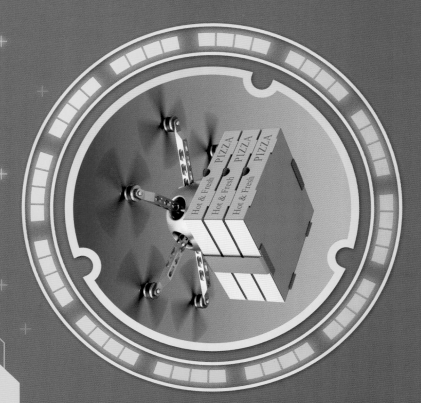

SKILLS AND QUALIFICATIONS:

| DRONE TECHNOLOGY | AT LEAST 16 YEARS OLD | ABLE TO PASS A TEST FROM THE FAA |

THERE'S A BUZZING SOUND HIGH IN THE SKY. You stand on your doorstep, watching as the mysterious flying object comes into sight. It's a drone, and it's delivering the pizza you ordered!

In the future, drones will likely be essential for future transportation, delivering goods and possibly even people from place to place. But that's not all: Future drones will keep tabs on growing crops and track down illegal poachers, too!

Drones are also called UAVs (unmanned aerial vehicles) because they fly without a pilot on board. But that doesn't mean there are no humans involved. Skilled human operators fly drones from on the ground. And in the future, this is one career that experts say is really going to take off.

JOB DESCRIPTION

In the future, experts predict that people will be needed to build drones, program them, and fly them. Already, drone pilots are using their aircraft to take aerial photos of houses to help owners sell them, keep tabs on construction projects, and create maps. In 2018, drones even delivered lifesaving vaccines to kids in Vanuatu, a remote island nation west of Fiji.

So far, concerns about safety have kept drones from flying in urban areas, where they might accidentally crash into houses, cars, or people. In 2016, Amazon made one customer's day when it delivered a TV streaming stick and a bag of popcorn using a drone. But it proved to be just a publicity stunt. Drone companies are still waiting on the United States' Federal Aviation Administration (FAA) to decide on rules about where, when, and how they'll be allowed to fly. Delivery company UPS hopes to have a fleet of delivery drones in the sky within the next few years.

WE OFFER:

- ☑ PAID TIME OFF
- ☑ A CHANCE TO SEE THE WORLD
- ☑ FREE PIZZA

APPLY TODAY!

Many experts think that soon, city skies will be full of delivery drones. Someday, they may even fly themselves. But in the near future, they'll need pilots.

SOUND INTERESTING?

Experts predict that drone technology could create more than 100,000 new jobs by 2025. Today, drone pilots need to be at least 16 years old and able to pass a test from the FAA to show knowledge about the rules of the sky. To prep people for careers in building, programming, and flying the more complex drones of the future, many universities around the country are beginning to offer college degrees focusing on drone technology.

HIGH FLYING
AIRLINES, UPGRADED

TODAY'S AIRPLANES HAVE YOU GRAPPLING FOR THE ARMREST WITH A STRANGER, WITH NOWHERE TO STRETCH YOUR CRAMPED LEGS AND NOTHING BUT A MEDIOCRE MICROWAVED MEAL TO BREAK UP THE ENDLESS TIME. BUT THOSE DISCOMFORTS COULD SOON BE IN THE PAST. AIRLINES ARE DEVELOPING NEW WAYS TO MAKE FLYING MORE FUN.

▶ SELF-CLEANING SEATS

There's nothing that ruins a nice vacation like getting sick on the plane ride there. So one aircraft seat manufacturer is developing a seat made of material that kills germs within seconds. As if keeping passengers healthy wasn't enough, the seats will give massages, too. Ahh.

◀ SUPER SPEED

Imagine being able to get from New York to London in 90 minutes instead of the normal seven hours. Most airliners fly at about 500 miles an hour (804 km/h). But in 2019, a new company called Hermeus announced plans to develop an aircraft that will someday travel at more than 3,000 miles an hour (4,828 km/h).

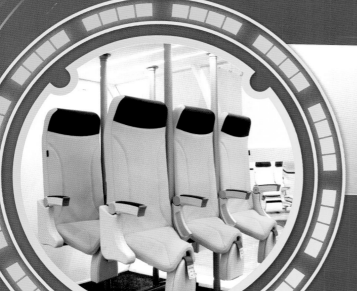

◀ STAND UP SEATING

Ok, this airline innovation definitely won't make flying more fun, but it could make room for more people. To cut costs, some airlines are experimenting with switching to "standing seats" that would cram in more passengers by having them perch on a bicycle-like seat. With your legs dangling on either side of the seat, it may seem a lot like riding a horse ... but way less fun. No thanks!

▼ A BAG WITH BRAINS

Future travelers stroll through an airport terminal, shopping for perfume and sunglasses as their luggage rolls along a few feet behind them. That's the idea behind Ovis, a smart suitcase that follows its owner through the airport. That's one less way to lose your bags!

▲ CHECK OUT

You're 10 hours into a 15-hour flight, and you've already finished your book and watched two movies. In the future, you might have a better boredom buster: A virtual reality helmet that can make you forget you're on a plane. You'll be so busy fighting aliens that the trip will be over in a snap!

FUTURE FAIL

WARP SPEED

◀ Superfast travel is commonplace in sci-fi franchises like *Star Trek* and *Star Wars*.

A PACK OF ENEMY SPACECRAFT LOOMS CLOSE, weapons ready to fire. You and your crew begin evasive maneuvers, but you can't shake the bad guys. You dodge one attack, then another. You've already pushed the throttle as far as it can go. There's only one option that could save your ship: engage hyperdrive mode! With the press of a button, your craft leaps forward, traveling faster than the speed of light. Warp speed is a staple space maneuver in all kinds of science fiction. But is it possible?

In 1947, test pilot Chuck Yeager accelerated an experimental, rocket-powered plane until a huge boom roared across the California desert below. He had become the first person to break the sound barrier, or travel faster than the speed of sound. (The loud noise was a sonic boom, created by the shock waves of his extreme speed.) Since then, people have dreamed of breaking another barrier: the speed of light. But according to Einstein's theory of relativity, nothing can travel faster than light. Some scientists theorize that it may be possible to get around Einstein's rule by warping space itself to make an object jump from one time to another. But for now, that's nothing more than a far-out theory.

▶ Warping space itself may sound extreme—and it is! Scientists theorize that supermassive objects, like black holes, can curve space-time.

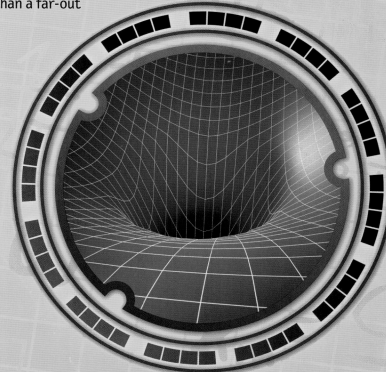

CHAPTER 3

🌍

GOING TO SPACE

THREE, TWO, ONE … BLASTOFF! HUMANS HAVE EXPLORED NEARLY EVERY CORNER OF PLANET EARTH, FROM THE TIP-TOPS OF MOUNTAINS TO THE BOTTOM OF THE DEEPEST CAVES. IN THE NEXT FEW DECADES, WE'LL TURN OUR SIGHTS ON NEW TERRITORY: OUTER SPACE. AS SOON AS THE 2030s, HUMANS COULD SET FOOT ON MARS—OUR FIRST JOURNEY TO ANOTHER PLANET. AND SCIENTISTS ARE COOKING UP PLANS TO SEND HIGH-TECH SPACECRAFT TO ALL KINDS OF OTHER EXCITING DESTINATIONS, FROM DISTANT MOONS TO NEIGHBORING SOLAR SYSTEMS.

SUIT UP

SPACE SUITS OF THE FUTURE

IN THE VAST, cold darkness of space, an astronaut floats, a thin tether all that keeps her from spinning away into nothingness. She's a fearless space explorer—but her oversize, white space suit makes her look more like an overpuffed marshmallow. Designers are working to change that, creating space gear as cool as the job it's designed for.

Traditional space suits are bulky and awkward. They are made of 14 layers of material and inflated with gas to protect astronauts from the harsh environment of space. For every video of astronauts bouncing around in the moon's low-gravity environment, there's another of astronauts tripping and falling face-first in their clumsy outfits. The balloon-like gloves make tasks that require working with the hands, such as spacecraft repairs, especially tricky. Could there be a superior suit?

Some experts think so, and they're hard at work creating one for future missions to Mars. One version is a skin-tight space suit that looks similar to a superhero's outfit. While a traditional, puffy space suit is filled with gas to simulate the pressure of Earth's atmosphere, the new space suit is a lightweight, stretchy garment lined with tiny coils. An astronaut would don the suit, then plug it in to the spacecraft's power supply to send a jolt of electricity through the coils, making them curl up and tighten the suit to the correct pressure. The sleek suit is still in development. But someday, a future astronaut could slip it on to explore the red planet—and beyond.

+ FUN FACT

A product designer created a concept for a space boot that could be made aboard a spacecraft using only human sweat and fungus spores.

+ FUN FACT

It takes 45 minutes to put on a traditional space suit.

▶ Space suits designed for exploration on Mars, such as NASA's Z-2 space suit, could look quite different from the space suits we're familiar with today.

WHO'S OUT THERE?

TOP PLACES IN THE UNIVERSE TO LOOK FOR LIFE

WHEN YOU LOOK UP INTO THE NIGHT SKY, HAVE YOU EVER WONDERED WHETHER SOMEONE IS LOOKING BACK?

▲TITAN

One nearby candidate for life is Titan, Saturn's largest moon. Besides Earth, it's the only known place in the solar system to have liquid lakes. They're not made of water, though—instead, they are filled with the liquid forms of the natural gases methane and ethane. These molecules contain the element carbon—an essential ingredient for life.

◀TRAPPIST-1 SYSTEM

Located 39 light-years away, a solar system much like our own floats through space. Around a small red star, about the size of Jupiter, there are seven rocky planets similar in size to Earth. Scientists think at least one of them could have liquid water on its surface, as well as oxygen, and perhaps even a climate similar to Earth's.

►K2-18B

In September 2019, astronomers announced the discovery of a new planet, K2-18b. It's a "super Earth" just over twice the size of our planet, and it's spinning through space right in the sweet spot of its star's habitable zone. What's more exciting: Scientists have detected liquid water there, the first time it's been found on any exoplanet. Some think it's the most exciting possible alien home yet discovered.

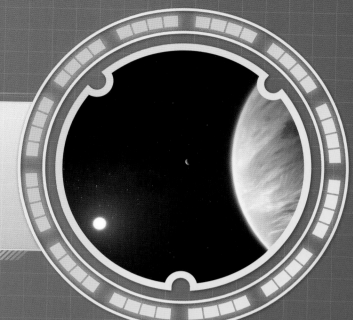

▼EUROPA

This moon of Jupiter is encased in an outer shell of ice estimated to be at least 10 miles (16 km) thick. But beneath that, it has an enormous ocean that covers the entire planet. Since all life as we know it needs water, scientists think Europa is one of the best places in the universe to check for life. Bonus: It's right in our own galactic neighborhood.

▲PROXIMA CENTAURI B

Just one solar system over from ours is Alpha Centauri, where three stars spin around each other. And orbiting one of those is a planet, Proxima Centauri b. It's about the size of Earth and exists in the "Goldilocks zone," what scientists call the swath of space that is just the right temperature to keep water in its liquid form. And Proxima Centauri b is just 4.24 light-years away—practically down the street in interstellar terms.

MISSION TO EUROPA

OCEAN MOON

LOCATED 390 MILLION MILES (628 MILLION KM) AWAY FROM EARTH, the moon Europa hangs in the blackness of space. Its icy surface, crisscrossed by strange reddish lines, is extremely reflective, making Europa seem to glow. And beneath all that bright ice is a vast ocean of warm, liquid water—perhaps the perfect place for life to grow. Scientists hope to go see for themselves as early as the 2020s.

GEARING UP

Already, five spacecraft have flown by Europa to check it out. The most recent, Galileo, orbited the host planet Jupiter between 1995 and 2003 and discovered evidence of Europa's enormous ocean. Now, NASA astronomers are at work on a new mission to get a close-up look at the moon. Called Europa Clipper, the mission is slated to launch as soon as 2023, then zip out to Jupiter and make about 40 close flybys over its mysterious moon.

Aboard the spacecraft will be nine instruments designed to answer scientists' most pressing questions about Europa. Among them: How thick is the ice? Does it have gaps that allow plumes of seawater to shoot into space? Do chunks of ice move along the surface? Answers to these questions will help clue in experts about what's going on in Europa's waters—and determine whether something could be swimming there.

HOME SWEET HOME?

A giant ocean trapped beneath a thick layer of ice might not seem like the best place to live. So why do experts think Europa may be home to alien life?

Europa could have all three of the ingredients required by life as we know it: water, chemical reactions, and energy. Water helps our cells dissolve nutrients and transports chemicals they need to stay alive.

Europa also has chemical reactions: Where its ice and its water meet, they could produce elements such as carbon, hydrogen, and oxygen. These elements could power the reactions living things depend on.

And Europa has energy: Interactions with Jupiter could create tides that produce heat. Experts think Europa may also have hydrothermal vents (openings in the seafloor that spew heated water rich in chemical nutrients from the planet's interior). While most life on Earth uses the heat of the sun for power, life on Europa could use this heat energy to survive.

DEEP DIVE

The Europa Clipper mission will fly just 15 miles (24 km) above the moon's surface—close enough to give scientists a clear view of the ice. But if there is something living on Europa, it will be hidden beneath that surface in its interior ocean. So one team at NASA hopes to not just zip by Europa but actually land on it. The Europa Lander is designed to touch down on the moon's icy surface, dig about four inches (10 cm) down, and analyze the sample material for signs of life. If chosen to fly, the Europa Lander could be part of the Clipper mission in the 2020s. If that goes well, astronomers hope to someday send a craft that can cut through the ice and launch a submarine into the moon's ocean. That craft will see if there's anything—or anyone—swimming in Europa's strange sea.

+ FUN FACT

Europa may have water geysers taller than Mount Everest.

GOING UP?

AN ELEVATOR TO SPACE

SENDING STUFF INTO ORBIT IS EXPENSIVE. Each pound of payload that blasts through Earth's atmosphere and into space costs about $10,000. But what if you could get supplies up there with no rocket required? That's the idea behind using a new kind of transportation system: the space elevator.

The idea of pushing an elevator's "up" button and climbing out of Earth's atmosphere might seem impossible. But experts say the idea is grounded in strong science. A tether made of extremely strong carbon nanotubes would stretch from Earth's surface to a space station held in place by Earth's gravity. The rotation of the Earth would keep the tether taut, allowing cars powered by solar energy to travel up and down its length.

The concept may be simple, but actually building an elevator to space is much more complicated. The tether would need to be nearly 60,000 miles (97,000 km) long, and the elevator would require materials that could withstand high-energy cosmic rays, collisions with debris, and other hazards of space. Not to mention that, at around $10 billion (U.S.), it would be one of the most expensive projects ever attempted in human history. But it could be worth the trouble: Experts estimate a space elevator would bring down the cost of lifting a payload into orbit to as low as $25 per pound.

In the future, astronauts could use the space elevator to transport not just people into space but entire spacecraft systems, such as engines, landing gear, and propellant. Spaceships could be constructed and launched from orbit, making it much easier to reach the moon, Mars, and the rest of the universe.

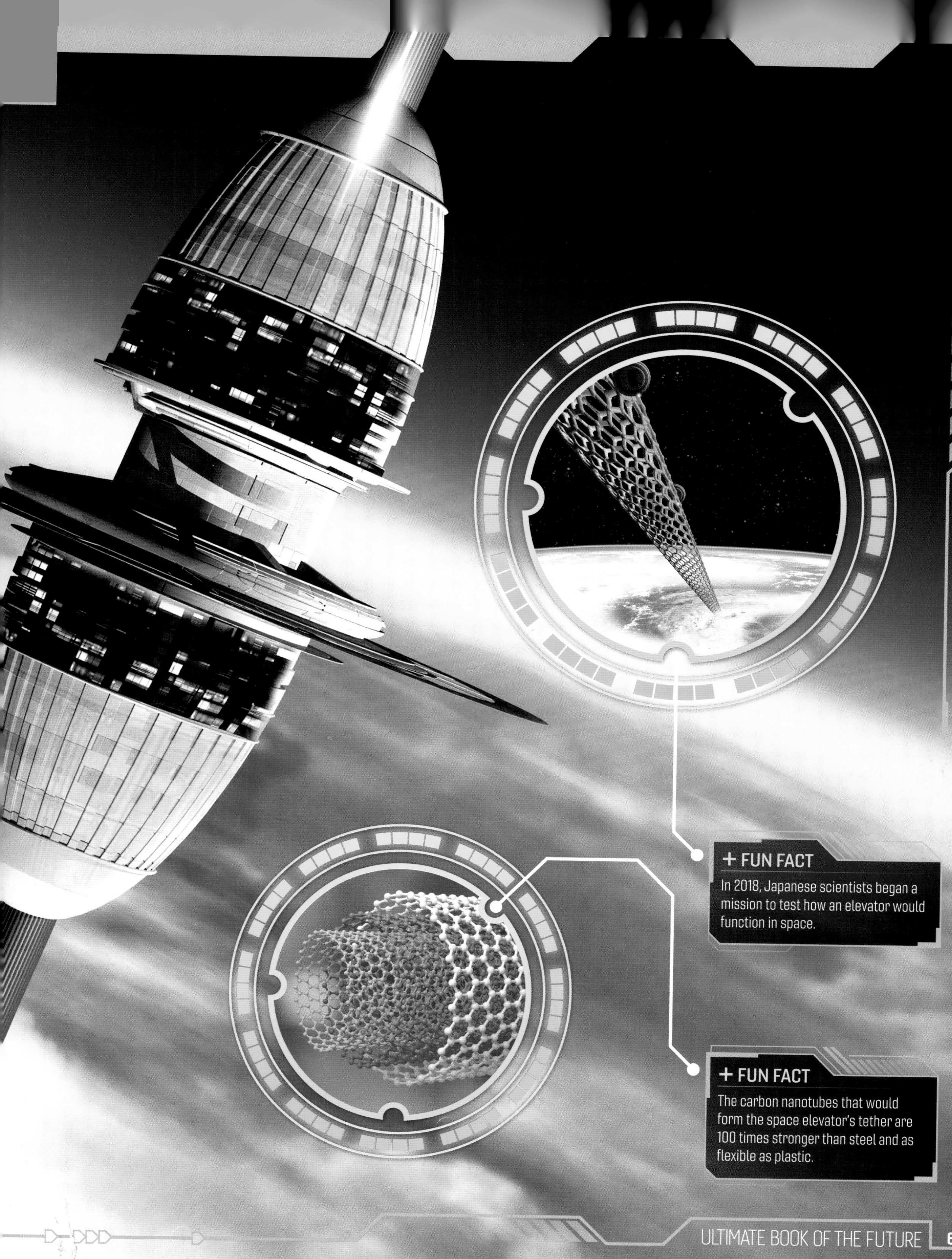

+ FUN FACT

In 2018, Japanese scientists began a mission to test how an elevator would function in space.

+ FUN FACT

The carbon nanotubes that would form the space elevator's tether are 100 times stronger than steel and as flexible as plastic.

LIFE ON MARS
✦ AT HOME ON THE RED PLANET

GET READY TO BLAST OFF! NASA hopes to send astronauts to Mars as early as the 2030s, when today's kids will be adults. That means you might be one of the first to strap in for the 140-million-mile (225-million-km) journey! Here's what life on a Mars colony might be like.

+ WATER WISE

Mars is drier than Earth's driest desert. So all gadgets on your space base will be designed to conserve every drop of water—even the toilets! In one prototype toilet, the same water from the bowl goes to the sink for you to wash your hands. If that sounds gross, don't worry—the water is filtered through a system that makes it clean enough to drink.

+ POWER UP

There's no food, water, or breathable air on Mars. So the first Martians (that's you!) will have to get creative. Solar panels might generate energy from the sun to power everything from your TV to heaters that keep you toasty during Mars's minus 100°F (-73°C) nights.

+ LANDING GEAR

Your first glimpse of your new home is through the tiny porthole window in your 1,000-square-foot (93-sq-m), gumdrop-shaped lander. As more landers touch down, inflatable tunnels connect them, creating a network of living spaces for the astronauts.

+ DRIVER'S SEAT

The entire red planet will be yours to explore. That means road trips that could last weeks. The last space vehicle that could carry humans, the Apollo Lunar Roving Vehicle from the 1970s, was a day-tripping buggy with space for two astronauts but no long-term supplies. Now a "space RV" currently in development has storage space for scientific equipment, benches for sleeping, a bathroom, and even a small kitchen.

+ MARS MENU

In 2014, astronauts on the International Space Station planted lettuce seeds in fertilizer-filled pillows, put them under LED lights, and carefully watered them. One month later, they ate the first space salad! Mars astronauts might someday grow their own fresh food in a Martian greenhouse.

THE FUTURE IS NOW

▶ MARS HELICOPTER

YOU MIGHT HAVE FLOWN A SMALL, remote-controlled helicopter for fun here on Earth. But imagine taking the same thing for a spin on the red planet. NASA's latest rover, Perseverance, had a sidekick—a helicopter named Ingenuity, ready to take to the Martian skies.

With its aerial view, a helicopter could gather information about what kind of terrain lies ahead, relaying it back to Earth so that the NASA crew can direct the rover toward interesting landmarks, and veer it away from places it could get stuck, such as sand traps. But creating the scout helicopter wasn't easy: Until 2021, no one had ever attempted to fly a craft on another world before.

On Earth, helicopters use their spinning rotor blades, which create an area of low-pressure, less dense air above that sucks the craft upward. But Mars's air is only one percent as dense as Earth's air. To make flying possible in those extreme conditions, the Mars helicopter has to be very small in size: Its body is about as big as a softball and weighs less than four pounds (1.8 kg). And the Mars chopper's blades spin at about 3,400 revolutions per minute—about 10 times as fast as a regular helicopter's blades.

Even with those challenges, Ingenuity was a success, flying longer than its original month-long mission. And it may be the first of many flying machines we send to check out other planets from above.

+ FUN FACT

Because it takes several minutes for information to travel the 140 million miles (225 million km) from Mars to Earth, helicopters will fly themselves.

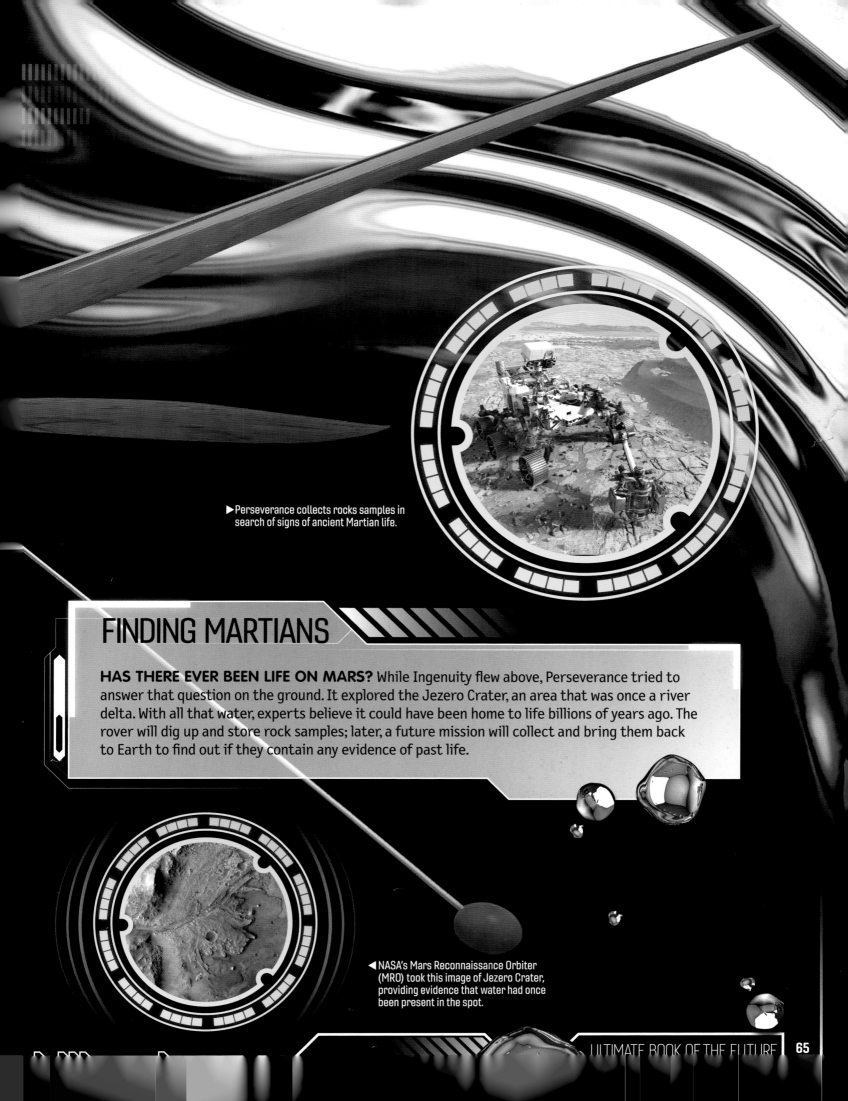

▶Perseverance collects rocks samples in search of signs of ancient Martian life.

FINDING MARTIANS

HAS THERE EVER BEEN LIFE ON MARS? While Ingenuity flew above, Perseverance tried to answer that question on the ground. It explored the Jezero Crater, an area that was once a river delta. With all that water, experts believe it could have been home to life billions of years ago. The rover will dig up and store rock samples; later, a future mission will collect and bring them back to Earth to find out if they contain any evidence of past life.

◀NASA's Mars Reconnaissance Orbiter (MRO) took this image of Jezero Crater, providing evidence that water had once been present in the spot.

SPACE BOTS

THIS IS A JOB FOR MACHINES

NOT ALL SPACE TASKS ARE FIT FOR HUMANS. SOME JOBS ARE TOO DANGEROUS, TOO DIRTY, OR JUST PLAIN DULL. THAT'S WHERE ROBOTS STEP IN. THESE MACHINES ARE DESIGNED TO BECOME ASTRONAUTS' RIGHT-HAND ROBOTS, TAKING OVER ROUTINE TASKS SO ASTRONAUTS CAN FOCUS ON THE IMPORTANT WORK, SUCH AS PERFORMING EXPERIMENTS—AND MAYBE, YOU KNOW, MEETING ALIENS.

On robot

GECKO GRIPPER

▶ CRAFTY CLIMBER

Mars is covered with cliffsides that scientists would love to get a close-up look at. By studying the layers of soil laid down over millions of years, they could read the cliffs to learn about the planet's history. But to reach them, they need something capable of scaling sheer wall faces. Enter the Gecko Gripper, a bot inspired by Earth's most skilled climber. The Gecko Gripper uses millions of tiny fibers to adhere to surfaces, the same strategy that enables the reptile to walk up walls.

◀ SUPERBOT

It might look like a superhero, but this robot is real: Named Valkyrie, it's NASA's newest humanoid robot. Standing 6 feet 2 inches (1.9 m) tall and wearing a glowing NASA logo on its chest, Valkyrie (Val for short) is designed to travel to new destinations, such as Mars, ahead of humans to set up the bases in advance.

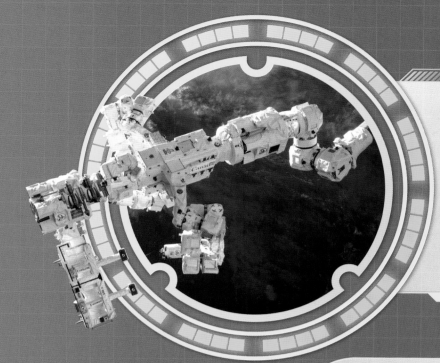

◀ THAT'S HANDY

When astronauts on the International Space Station (ISS) climb onto the outside of the craft to do repairs, they sometimes need an extra hand. Luckily, Dextre has two. This robot (full name: Special Purpose Dextrous Manipulator) is attached to the exterior of the ISS, looking like a gigantic torso with two 11-foot (3.5-m) arms. Dextre performs routine maintenance—and even has his own workbench for fixing equipment!

▼ DIG DEEP

In 2018, NASA landed a new kind of rover on Mars. While past rovers have motored their way across the red planet, this one, called InSight, is doing something different—staying in place. From its position on the Elysium Planitia region of Mars, it is using a small probe nicknamed "the mole" to dig beneath Mars's dusty surface until it hits bedrock. It will take measurements to help clue scientists into what the interior of Mars is made of.

▲ WHAT A BUZZ

In 2019, NASA sent three robots into space. Called the Astrobees, they are cube-shaped robots that live aboard the International Space Station, where their job is to work alongside astronauts. The Astrobees—named Honey, Queen, and Bumble, use electric fans to fly around their zero-gravity environment, monitoring equipment and keeping track of supplies.

[COULD IT HAPPEN?]

▶ COULD AN ASTEROID DESTROY EARTH?

SIXTY-SIX MILLION YEARS AGO, a bright light appeared in the sky above North America. It was an asteroid six miles (10 km) across, and it was headed straight toward Earth. When it slammed into our planet at 45,000 miles an hour (72,000 km/h), it gouged a crater 18 miles (29 km) deep and released energy equivalent to more than a billion atomic bombs. About 75 percent of all living organisms on Earth—including most of the dinosaurs—disappeared. What if another asteroid was on a collision course with Earth?

EYES ON THE SKY

The dinosaurs were taken by surprise when that asteroid struck. But humans won't be. That's because a team of scientists are continuously scanning the sky for fast-moving objects. Because most asteroids and smaller meteorites burn up when they pass through Earth's atmosphere (we call them shooting stars for the streaks of light they create), the asteroid-hunters focus on bigger space rocks. So far, they have found and tracked about 95 percent of rocks big enough to end civilization—those more than 0.6 mile (1 km) wide.

Most potentially dangerous objects come from the asteroid belt, a disk-shaped formation located between the orbits of Mars and Jupiter. It's made up of rock bits left over from the formation of the solar system. Scientists are already tracking all the potentially deadly asteroids floating there, and there are none on track to hit Earth. But it is possible that a giant comet or an asteroid dislodged from its orbit could be coming for us undetected. Scientists might not spot that object until it is between the orbits of Uranus and Neptune— about 20 years before it reaches us. Then, it would be time to step into action.

◀ NASA's Wide-field Infrared Survey Explorer (WISE) scans the sky for asteroids and comets.

SAVING EARTH

We'd likely know an asteroid was heading our way decades before impact. That would give the people of planet Earth plenty of time to band together and deflect the killer rock. Experts have all kinds of ideas about how to do that. A few: Tug it out of the way with a spacecraft, use heat from the sun to redirect it, zap it with a laser, or blast it with a nuclear warhead.

Blowing up the space rock might sound cool, but experts say the best way to get an asteroid out of the way is with a gentle nudge. That's because if an asteroid is broken into pieces, those pieces will continue flying through space—and one of them could strike our planet. Oops. In 2019, NASA announced plans to test the idea by launching a spacecraft into Didymos, a nearby asteroid system. Didymos is a 2,600-foot (800-m) asteroid orbited by a small moon that will come within about seven million miles (11 million km) of Earth in 2022. The test will let scientists study how to successfully knock an asteroid off course—so that if the big one is headed our way, they can save our planet.

What do you think is the best way to take down a monster space rock?

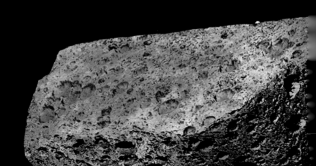

SPACE PILOT

EDUCATION:
ENGINEERING, MATH, PHYSICS, OR A RELATED FIELD

SKILLS AND QUALIFICATIONS:
FORMER TEST PILOT   ABILITY TO WORK WELL WITH CREW AND PASSENGERS

IF YOU'VE EVER THOUGHT THAT YOU MIGHT WANT TO BE AN ASTRONAUT SOMEDAY, you're in luck: In the future, planet Earth will need a whole lot more of these high-flying folks.

In humanity's first 50 years of venturing beyond our own planet, space programs run by governments put people into orbit around Earth and set them down to stroll on the moon. Experts believe that spacefaring will undergo a big shift in the next 50 years: Government organizations like NASA will switch their focus to sending astronauts to Mars and asteroids—leaving private companies in charge of near-Earth operations. Along with supplying the International Space Station, those companies plan to send tourists who want a truly far-out trip into space. All that will mean a big demand for pilots with the right stuff.

JOB DESCRIPTION

Private companies are already ramping up plans to allow tourists to experience the thrill of space travel. To date, Virgin Galactic has sold more than 700 tickets to would-be space tourists for between $200,000 and $250,000 a pop. In 2018, they started running test flights, taking their spaceplane, the VSS Unity, 51 miles (82 km) above Earth's surface—to the very edge of space. Soon, they plan to take six tourists at a time up in a U-shaped flight that will curve above Earth's atmosphere, allowing them to experience several minutes of weightlessness and take photos of Earth from high above. Then, the plane will land on the runway, ready for the next tourist group to board.

WE OFFER:

 HIGH-FLYING ADVENTURE

 SLEEP ABOARD THE ISS

The International Space Station will soon open its airlocks to tourists, too. In 2019, NASA announced that soon, passengers will be able to shell out $35,000 per night for a far-out hotel experience: sleeping aboard the ISS. The station will have room for two paying guests to stay for as long as a month. Visitors will book a ride with SpaceX or another company.

As space tourism takes flight, companies will need pilots to command the rockets and space-planes that will take visitors to their galactic destinations. And one of them could be you.

SOUND INTERESTING?

Space pilots will need strong flying skills and an ability to work well with crew and passengers. Virgin Galactic recruits former test pilots—aircraft pilots with extra training who test out new or experimental planes. Test pilots need a degree in engineering, math, physics, or a related field. After that, most serve as military pilots and then attend test-pilot school.

FUTURE FAIL.

MISSION TO ALPHA CENTAURI

◀◀◀

HUMANS ARE OUT TO COLONIZE SPACE
in the 1960s TV show (and the 2018 remake)
Lost in Space. Their first stop? Alpha Centauri,
the star system closest to Earth. Alpha
Centauri has a lot going for it as a potential
host for humanity: It's only 4.3 light-years
away, right down the street in intergalactic
terms. And in 2017, astronomers announced
evidence that the star system is home to several exoplanets that look friendly to human life.
But for the wannabe Alpha Centaurians in *Lost in
Space,* things don't go so well (that's what gives the
show its name). And as for us Earthings, a trip to Alpha
Centauri isn't looking so good either.

▲ The 1960s TV show *Lost in Space*
followed a family of colonists
trying to survive in space.

Alpha Centauri may be close compared to other intergalactic destinations, but it's still far away—really far. A
span of 4.3 light-years might sound like just a blip, but it equates to more than
25.6 trillion miles. It would take a space shuttle about 165,000
years to reach it—so long that a human astronaut could
not come close to making it in a lifetime. But Alpha
Centauri is still our best bet for exploring a solar
system outside of our own. One mission, called
Breakthrough Starshot, hopes to explore it using a
fleet of teeny-tiny spacecraft accelerated by
lasers to superspeed, which could reach the system within the century. Pretty cool—but nothing
like an intergalactic human space colony.

FAIL.

▲ The Breakthrough Starshot program aims
to send tiny, stamp-size chips into space.

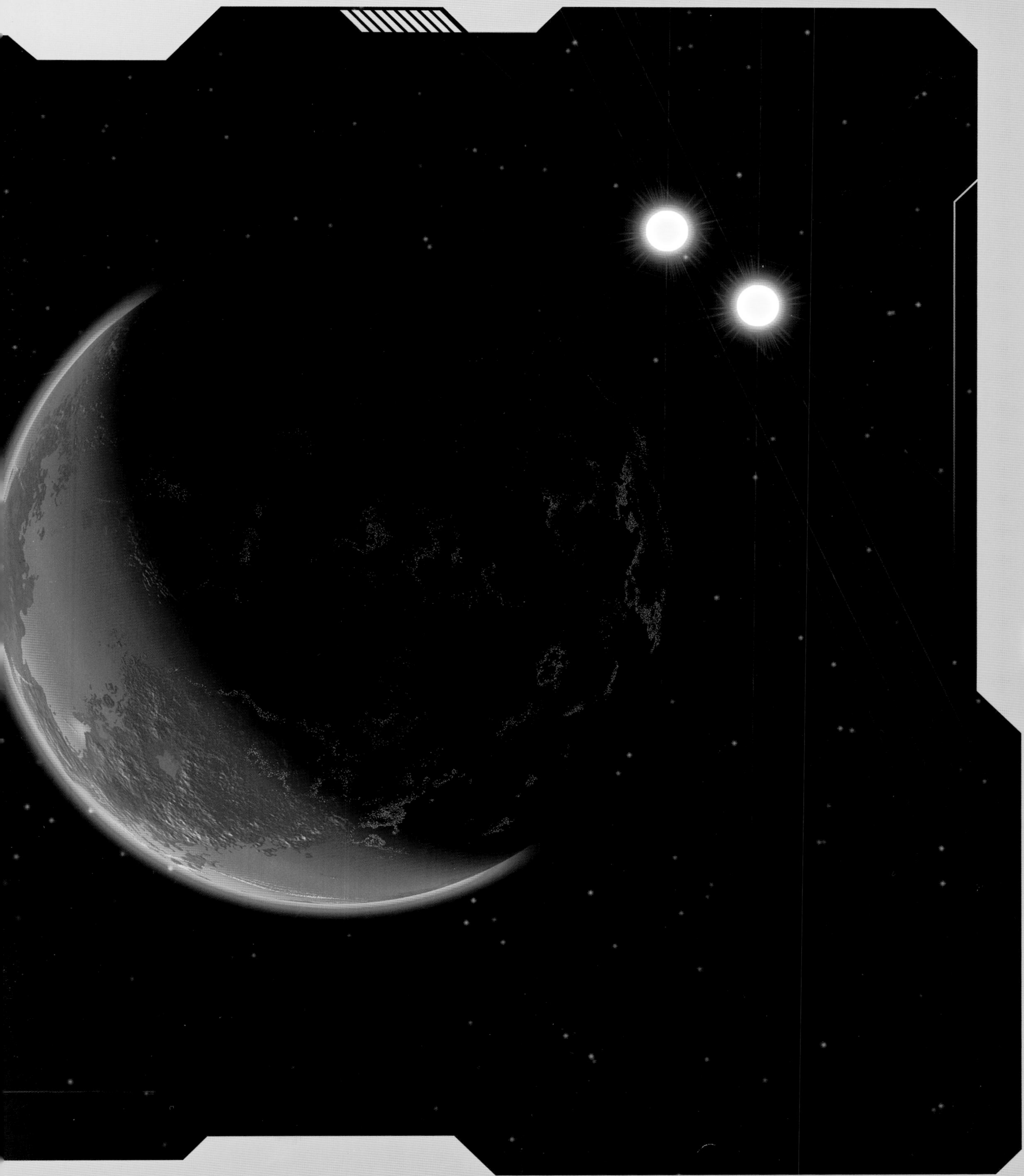

CHAPTER 4 🌍

SAVING THE WORLD

EARTH IS FACING PROBLEMS THAT CAN MAKE THE FUTURE SEEM SCARY. THE PLANET IS WARMING, TRASH IS PILING UP, AND THE WORLD'S POPULATION IS SKYROCKETING—JUST TO NAME A FEW. HERE'S THE GOOD NEWS: MANY EXPERTS BELIEVE THAT SOLUTIONS TO THESE PROBLEMS AND OTHERS ARE WITHIN OUR GRASP. ACROSS THE GLOBE, SCIENTISTS ARE HARD AT WORK DESIGNING INVENTIONS AND DEVELOPING TECHNOLOGIES TO SOLVE THEM. FROM SMART STRUCTURES TO SMART ROBOTS, HERE'S HOW FUTURE TECH COULD SAVE THE WORLD.

COOL DOWN
✛ WACKY TECH VS. GLOBAL WARMING

PLANET EARTH IS HEATING UP. Humans rely on cars and factories powered by burning fossil fuels, such as coal, oil, and gas. The resulting gases are released into the air, where they act like an invisible blanket, holding in heat from the sun and causing the planet's temperature to rise. The best way to stop it: Curb use of fossil fuels and switch to green sources of energy, like wind and water power. But that practical option hasn't stopped scientists from dreaming of other ways to help. Here are some of their zaniest—and brainiest—alternatives, last-ditch ideas to stopping global warming in its tracks.

✛ PAINTING MOUNTAINS

Glaciers—those vast sheets of ice at Earth's poles—help cool the planet down. That's because their white color reflects light and heat from the sun back out toward space and away from our planet. This is called the albedo effect. But as Earth warms because of climate change, glacier ice melts, reducing the albedo effect and heating up the planet even more. A group of concerned citizens in Peru is trying to combat the big melt with a simple solution: painting a mountain, called Chalon Sombrero—once home to a healthy glacier—bright white. They hope the paint job will restore the albedo effect and help the glacier regrow. If it works, it could be a low-cost way to combat climate change.

✛ OCEAN GROWING

Carbon dioxide is one of the greenhouse gases that holds in heat and warms the planet. Luckily, there are creatures on Earth with an appetite for the stuff. Phytoplankton (microscopic, plant-like creatures that live in the ocean) suck harmful carbon dioxide out of the air. What if we gave them a helping hand? Scientists have experimented with dumping iron, an element phytoplankton need to grow, into one location in the ocean. The result was a huge growth of hungry phytoplankton that gobbled up the carbon dioxide, causing levels in the area to drop. Still, some researchers are skeptical of the approach and its potential side effects.

+ CREATING CLOUDS

On June 15, 1991, Mount Pinatubo in the Philippines erupted, sending a cloud of volcanic ash hundreds of miles across into the sky. The cloud had an unexpected effect: It formed a sunshield that reflected some of the sun's energy back into space, lowering Earth's temperature by one degree Fahrenheit (0.6 degree Celsius). That made experts wonder: Could we replicate the event on purpose to counteract global warming? Scientists are experimenting with a system for spraying sea salt high into the sky. There, water vapor would collect on the particles of salt, forming clouds that would help reflect the sun's heat back into space. But once started, the process would have to go on forever, or the planet would rewarm rapidly.

+ SPACE UMBRELLA

When you get too hot at the beach, you put up an umbrella—so why not do the same for the planet? It sounds impossible, but scientists estimate we would only need to diminish the sun's glare by 2 to 4 percent to get the planet's temperature back to normal. Experts have different ideas about how to do this, but one is a fleet of trillions of butterfly-size robots that would come together to form a sunshade 60,000 miles (97,000 km) wide. But how to launch them is a puzzle—not to mention the small problem that the technology doesn't exist yet.

TRASH THE TRASH

TECH THAT TAKES OUT THE GARBAGE

THE AVERAGE AMERICAN CREATES ABOUT 130 POUNDS (59 KG) OF WASTE A MONTH. ALL OVER THE WORLD, WASTE PILES UP IN LANDFILLS AND CLOGS RIVERS AND OCEANS. AND SCIENTISTS ESTIMATE THAT BY 2100, WE'LL BE PRODUCING THREE TIMES AS MUCH TRASH AS WE ARE NOW: 11 MILLION TONS (10 MILLION T) A DAY. HERE ARE FOUR INVENTIONS THAT MIGHT HELP US CLEAN UP OUR ACT.

◄ SAVE OUR SEAS

In the waters between the U.S. states of California and Hawaii is a collection of trash about twice the size of Texas. Called the Great Pacific Garbage Patch, it contains about 1.8 trillion pieces of trash. Cleaning up that floating landfill has been the dream of Dutch inventor Boyan Slat since he was in high school. His invention is a 200-foot (600-m)-long floating tube with a "skirt" that dangles beneath. Wind, waves, and currents carry trash into the system, where it is corralled. Then, a ship can collect it and take it back to shore to be recycled into new products. Slat's Ocean Cleanup launched in 2018, where it ran into technical problems. But Slat didn't give up. Since then, his team has improved the design multiple times, and, in 2020, they created their first product made from recycled garbage patch plastic: sunglasses.

◀ DISAPPEARING ACT

When cell phones, computers, and tablets stop working, they often get tossed in the trash. Worldwide, people dump around 45 million tons (41 million t) of electronic waste into landfills every year. There, components inside the devices pollute the air, water, and soil. So engineers at Stanford University in California decided to rethink how electronics are made. They created a new type of material that could be easily dissolved. After a month in regular vinegar, it disappears. Someday, electronics made from this material could simply vanish when we're through with them.

▼ WASTE WATER

When on vacation with his family, Ohio, U.S.A., teen Luke Clay was stunned by the sight of beautiful beaches covered in garbage. Even worse, most of the litter was Styrofoam, which can take up to 500 years to break down. So Clay, along with two classmates, became determined to find a solution. A few years later, the trio had invented a process to turn Styrofoam trash into carbon, then use that to make water filters. The creation not only reduces Styrofoam waste, it also helps provide clean water to the 663 million people in the world without it.

▲ CAN DO

An astounding amount of trash enters the ocean every year—the equivalent of five full garbage bags of waste stacked on top of each other on every foot (30 cm) of coastline around the world. Much of it enters the water at the shore, where it breaks down into smaller and smaller pieces. But what if we could collect it first? Two surfers from Australia designed a device called the Seabin that works like a floating garbage can. A cylinder rests below the sea surface, with a pump at the bottom that sucks water in, and a filter that collects the trash. Seabins have already been installed at some ports and marinas around the world.

COULD IT HAPPEN?

▶ COULD ALL OF EARTH'S ICE MELT?

THERE ARE MORE THAN 326 MILLION TRILLION GALLONS (1,234 MILLION TRILLION L) OF WATER ON EARTH. More than two-thirds of it is frozen in glaciers and ice caps. As climate change warms the planet, this ice is melting away. In parts of the world, the shift is dramatic: In Glacier National Park, Montana, U.S.A., there were about 150 glaciers in 1910. Today, there are fewer than 30. And scientists estimate that all the rest could be gone within 30 years. If climate change isn't stopped, more and more of Earth's ice will melt. Could all of it disappear—and what would happen if it did?

WATER WORLD

If the planet continues to warm, the ice could indeed continue to melt until it's all gone. Fortunately, there is so much ice on Earth that scientists estimate that it would take 5,000 years to melt completely, giving people a long time to deal with the challenges of a changing planet. And if humans are able to slow the burning of fossil fuels, there's still time to curb climate change.

An ice-free Earth would be much warmer, with an average temperature around 80°F (27°C) instead of the current 58°F (14°C). And it wouldn't just feel different: It would look totally different, too.

The meltwater would flood into the world's oceans, raising the sea level by 216 feet (66 m). Coastlines all around the world would change shape: In North America, Florida and the Atlantic seaboard would disappear, the hills of San Francisco would become small islands, and the Gulf of California would swallow up San Diego. In Europe, places such as London, Venice, and the Netherlands would disappear. Australia would have a new sea in its center. Antarctica would almost entirely vanish underwater.

LIFE AT THE LIMITS

Earth's living things would have big changes to deal with. Arctic and Antarctic animals—such as polar bears, reindeer, snowy owls, narwhals, and walruses—would lose their habitats. Elsewhere, animals would be faced with changes in the terrain, seasons, and plant life they depend on for food. Some would adapt, moving north to cooler areas, changing their migration patterns, and finding new sources of food. But many would not be able to change with the changing planet.

Humans would face big changes, too. Half of the people in the world currently live on the coasts. Billions of people would find themselves without a home. As the seas warmed, currents would shift, changing weather patterns around the globe: Some places, like Africa, would become so warm that much of its land would be impossible to live on. Other places, like Europe, would become much colder.

How do you think people should deal with Earth's melting ice?

▲ INSET (THEN):
Mount Gould, roughly a hundred years ago, when Glacier National Park, U.S.A., was covered in considerably more ice than it is now

▶ MAIN IMAGE (NOW):
Mount Gould, a peak in Glacier National Park, as it stands today

RESCUE ROBOTS

GOING WHERE HUMANS CAN'T

DURING DISASTERS, BUILDINGS COLLAPSE, FIRES BURN, AND THE AIR AND WATER BECOME UNSAFE. FOR WEEKS AND MONTHS AFTERWARD, EMERGENCY ZONES ARE HAZARDOUS. YET, THERE'S WORK TO DO: TOXIC CHEMICALS NEED TO BE CONTAINED, FIRES PUT OUT, AND, SOMETIMES, VICTIMS NEED TO BE RESCUED. IT'S A JOB TOO DANGEROUS FOR HUMANS. ENTER THE ROBOTS.

▶ HORSE SENSE

Four legs give a robot stability, but two arms make it able to operate in an environment built for humans. So why not combine the two? That's what robotics engineers from the Italian Institute of Technology did with their bot: Similar to the mythical centaur, their Centauro robot has four wheeled lower limbs attached to a humanoid torso with two arms. Centauro can reconfigure its legs to move over obstacles, lift objects, and even karate-chop wood planks in two.

◀ BUG BOT

It can fly, land on walls, and then scurry across them. No, it's not an insect: it's SCAMP, a robot designed at Stanford University. SCAMP (Stanford Climbing and Aerial Maneuvering Platform) is designed to zip into places such as earthquake zones, where there are no flat surfaces for a traditional drone to touch down. To create it, robotics engineers mimicked a housefly's manner of maneuvering to fly, perch, climb, and recover from slips. Once deployed in a disaster zone, SCAMP could measure conditions or set up a temporary communications network.

◀ROACH ROBOT

Cockroaches can withstand being squished by pressure 900 times their body weight and squeeze through gaps just .12 inch (3 mm) wide, barely thicker than pencil lead. As a result, there is almost nowhere roaches can't go. Researchers thought they'd be the ideal critter to mimic for a disaster robot capable of crawling through rubble and fallen buildings. So they designed a cockroach-inspired robot that can compress its outer shell to lower its height by half—and keep on crawling.

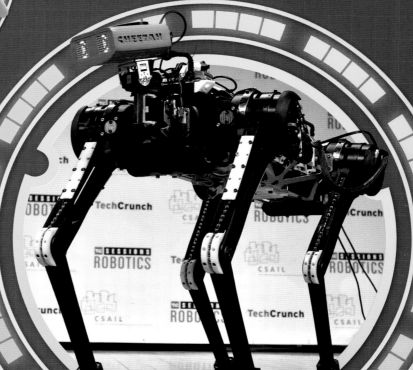

▶CATLIKE REFLEXES

Cheetah is a 90-pound (40.8-kg), four-legged bot developed by the Massachusetts Institute of Technology (MIT), U.S.A., that can gallop 13 feet (4 m) per second across rough terrain, climb stairs covered with obstacles, and leap onto a desk. It does all this blind; instead of using cameras to sense its environment, it feels its way around like a person navigating a pitch-dark room. Scientists think Cheetah could be ideal for locating people in disaster areas.

◀WATER BOT

Not all natural disasters happen on land. Events like floods, oil spills, or nuclear power plant breakdowns can create dangerous water conditions. The Robotics Institute at Carnegie Mellon University in Pennsylvania, U.S.A., has the answer: a boat-like bot called Platypus meant to navigate through waterways. Platypus uses onboard sensors to measure things like pH, oxygen, temperature, and depth. When they needed to measure the pollution of Kenya's Mara River, scientists sent Platypus, disguised as a crocodile to keep aggressive hippos from attacking it.

FLAMEOUT

FIGHTING FIRES WITH SOUND

EVERY YEAR, more than 100,000 wildfires rage in the United States alone, burning up between four and five million acres (1.6 to 2 million ha). Raging wildfires can move at speeds of up to 14 miles an hour (23 km/h), swallowing up trees, brush, homes, and everything else in their path. Battling these fires is hot, dirty, dangerous work. But what if firefighters could use something as simple as sound to put out the flames?

In 2017, two engineering students named Seth Robertson and Viet Tran invented what might be the fire extinguisher of the future. Traditionally, firefighters either douse fires with water or spray them with chemical retardants to stop the burning. But the new device uses neither. Instead, it emits sound to put out fires. Sound moves in waves that vibrate what they're passing through. That vibration can be enough to separate the flames from the oxygen they need to burn, putting the fire out. Robertson and Tran

+ FUN FACT

Earth is the only known planet where there is enough oxygen for a fire to burn.

+ FUN FACT

Ancient humans harnessed the power of fire about 400,000 years ago.

rigged up an amplifier and a cardboard tube to focus the sound. When they blasted low-frequency tones through their "sonic extinguisher," flames went out.

Now, Robertson and Tran are working on turning their prototype into a real-life product. They think the technology could be ideal for putting out small fires in the home: A sonic extinguisher could be installed over a stove top to extinguish kitchen fires, for example. Someday, drones equipped with sonic extinguishers could fight forest fires without needing to refill water or retardant and without putting human lives in danger. And a sound-based device could be extremely useful in space, where zero gravity makes it impossible to spray a traditional fire extinguisher. Now that's a sound idea.

THE FUTURE IS NOW

▶ BUILDINGS MADE OF TRASH

LOOK AROUND YOU. Do you see anything—the floor, the walls—that is made of recycled material? Probably not. But in the future, that could change. One engineer envisions a tomorrow in which we're all living in buildings made of material that was once in the garbage pile.

To make that happen, engineer Arthur Huang created the Trashpresso, a portable recycling center that turns plastic trash into tiles that can be used for building. Designed to fit inside a 40-foot (12-m) shipping container, Trashpresso can be hauled anywhere in the world. Then, it uses solar power to wash, shred, melt, and mold plastic trash into usable material. The tiles it creates can be used for floors and walls.

Recycling plastic waste uses just 20 percent of the energy that it takes to manufacture new plastic. Ideally, we would use no plastic at all, says Huang. But even if we can get to that point, there is still 100 years' worth of plastic clogging landfills on Earth. Recycling it into buildings is a step in the right direction. Huang's company, Miniwiz, develops all kinds of technology for turning waste into something usable. It has invented a new material, Natrilon, a kind of yarn made from plastic bottles and rice husks—and it created a concept store for Nike in Shanghai, China, built completely out of materials made from recycled bottles, cans, and DVDs. Huang envisions a future in which trash is turned not just into buildings but also into clothing, boats, and even airplanes.

YOU CAN HELP!

EVERY LITTLE BIT COUNTS. HERE ARE 10 WAYS YOU CAN REDUCE YOUR PLASTIC USE.

1. Switch to paper or metal straws.
2. Carry a reusable water bottle.
3. Pack lunch in a reusable container.
4. Snack on fruit—it's healthy and needs no packaging!
5. Encourage your family to buy staples like cereal, pasta, and rice from bulk bins.
6. Store leftovers in glass containers instead of plastic bags or wrap.
7. Avoid face wash, toothpaste, and other products that contain microbeads, tiny bits of plastic that can end up in the ocean. (Hint: Avoid the ingredients polyethylene or polypropylene.)
8. Shop your local farmers market: Local fruits and veggies have a low carbon footprint and no plastic packaging.
9. Choose a cone: Ice cream eaten this way has no waste—sweet!
10. Pick up after others. Clean up trash whenever you see it, and leave the world a better place.

▶ Huang's machine turns used plastic into tiles.

▲ Trashpresso is a portable recycling plant, powered by solar panels.

SAVING SPECIES

TECH TO PROTECT

ALL AROUND PLANET EARTH, animals leap, hop, and flap. From desert foxes that spend their days snoozing under hot sand to polar bears spending a lifetime on frozen ice, all kinds of critters share our home. Unfortunately, as humans expand into all corners of the globe, many species are struggling to survive. Experts estimate that as many as 20,000 creatures are on the brink of extinction. But there's hope: Around the world, people are working to save these animals. And now, they've got new high-tech tools to help them get the job done.

KEEPING TRACK

Earth is a big place. Scientists traipse through jungles and trek up mountains in search of new species, but they are still not close to knowing everything that's out there. Some experts have estimated that 81 percent of all animals, plants, and fungi are still undiscovered.

With the majority of species still unknown, it's hard for scientists to figure out which are in danger of going extinct. Luckily, tech is helping us map our planet with

extreme accuracy. You might use Google Earth to get directions, but scientists use the technology to protect animals. Already, they've accomplished a lot simply by clicking around: One group found an unmapped rainforest in Mozambique. When they went to explore the area on foot, they discovered three new species of butterfly and one snake previously unknown to science.

Other groups are combining mapping technology with another tool: satellite tracking. They can outfit an animal with a "smart"

◄ This robo-chick blends right into a penguin colony.

collar that tracks the critter's location and shows how and where it's moving. That helps biologists predict animals' behavior and know which areas they depend on for food and shelter. One group, called Save the Elephants, uses mapping and tracking to monitor the movements of endangered African elephants so they can figure out which areas need to be protected to help the animals survive.

UP CLOSE AND PERSONAL

Traditionally, keeping tabs on wild animals is difficult and dirty work. Scientists regularly wade through swamps and dig in the mud to get close enough to cautious critters to study them. And if that isn't tough enough, getting information about animals' health often involves collecting and analyzing their poo! But new advances in technology means that robots can now take over some of these tasks.

Collecting a blood sample from a blue whale the length of a 747 airplane is no easy feat. In the past, scientists have only been able to get that information from dead or stranded whales. But in 2010, they got creative: They strapped petri dishes to a remote-controlled helicopter and flew them through the spray of a whale's spout. That spray contains mucus—whale snot—that the team analyzed for bacteria to get an idea of the whale's health.

Emperor penguins are shy animals. When they sense humans are nearby, they'll keep far away, making observing them tough. So international scientists came up with a way to get a bird's-eye view of the penguins—literally. They created a remote-controlled, wheeled robot dressed up as a fluffy penguin chick and sent it rolling right into the colony. The disguise was so convincing, adult penguins sang to the robo-chick!

Technology will surely be a big part of future life. But it doesn't just make our lives easier—it could help make sure the animals we share our planet with have better lives, too.

SAVING THE WORLD

MIND READER

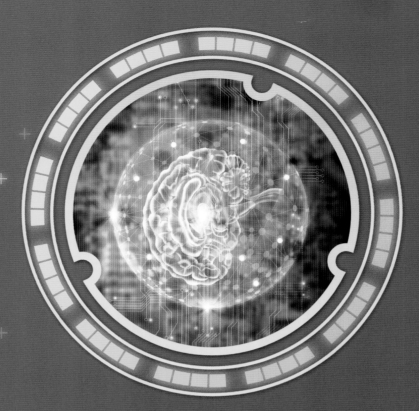

WE OFFER:

 MEANINGFUL WORK

 ON-THE-JOB TRAINING

SKILLS AND QUALIFICATIONS:

A BACKGROUND IN NEUROSCIENCE OR ARTIFICIAL INTELLIGENCE

COMPUTER PROGRAMMING

YOU READ THAT RIGHT: MIND READER. Scientists have been able to read people's brain wave patterns for decades. EEG (electroencephalogram) machines, for example, use small metal disks attached to the scalp to detect and track electrical activity in the brain. Those brain waves can help doctors diagnose illnesses, but scientists haven't had a way to interpret them to figure out what someone is thinking—until now.

New technology is making it possible to get a whole new view into the human mind. And in the future, a host of experts will have jobs in the field of thought interpretation. The possibilities of the new tech are nearly endless, and could help solve many of the problems of the future.

JOB DESCRIPTION

Today, a new field of neuroscience is beginning to decode brain waves to reveal the inner workings of the mind. Some computer programs can already monitor people's brain waves as they look at faces, then draw those same faces on a computer, re-creating them directly from the person's thoughts. Other programs are learning to interpret the brain waves of people who can't speak and create audio of their thoughts that plays out of a speaker.

These technologies can improve human life in all kinds of ways. People who have been paralyzed could use thought-interpretation technology to control bionic limbs that they can use to eat, climb, and run simply by thinking. And the tech could come in handy as Earth's population explodes in the future: Older people who have trouble speaking after suffering strokes could

☑ PSYCHIC POWERS
(NOT REALLY)

APPLY TODAY!

switch to communicating through computers. And travelers in foreign countries could use brain-reading tech to communicate in unfamiliar languages. All of these technologies have to be researched, built, and tested by knowledgeable humans. Maybe one of them will be you.

SOUND INTERESTING?

Brain wave analysts of the future will need backgrounds in brain science and artificial intelligence. Focus on biology to learn about how the mind works or study computer programming to learn how to shape artificial intelligence programs. This future field will need smart and creative people who are excited about using technology to improve lives.

FUTURE FAIL

FORCE FIELDS ▽

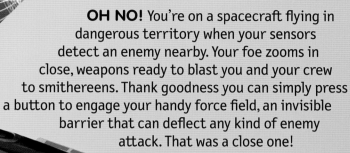

OH NO! You're on a spacecraft flying in dangerous territory when your sensors detect an enemy nearby. Your foe zooms in close, weapons ready to blast you and your crew to smithereens. Thank goodness you can simply press a button to engage your handy force field, an invisible barrier that can deflect any kind of enemy attack. That was a close one!

Not so fast. It would be great if we had force fields to protect ourselves from harm during car accidents or shield the planet from an interplanetary attack. But this is one sci-fi technology that we're still waiting for. In 2015, aircraft manufacturer Boeing filed a patent, or plan, for a system designed to prevent explosion shock waves from hitting a target. According to the patent, a sensor would detect an explosion, signaling lasers, electricity, and microwaves to produce a shield made of plasma (the same stuff that makes up the sun). The only problem? Just because a company has plans for such a device doesn't mean they know how to build it. And even if it's possible, Boeing's device might be able to prevent the shock wave from an explosion reaching a target, but it wouldn't do anything to stop physical objects, like bullets or shrapnel. That's not much of a force field.

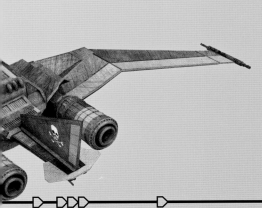

CHAPTER 5 🌍
OUT AND ABOUT

ALL AROUND YOU, SKYSCRAPERS STRETCH UPWARD. THEIR WALLS ARE SLEEK GLASS DOTTED WITH AREAS OF LUSH GREEN—VERTICAL GARDENS GROWING ON THEIR SIDES, HIGH ABOVE THE GROUND. YOU HEAR A WHIRRING NOISE ABOVE: DRONES OVERHEAD, DELIVERING PACKAGES AND TRANSPORTING PEOPLE. YOUR STOMACH RUMBLES, SO YOU STOP AT A FOOD STAND TENDED BY A ROBOT CHEF FOR YOUR FAVORITE SNACK—A HOT DOG MADE FROM MEAT GROWN IN A LAB. IT'S AN AVERAGE DAY HERE IN THE YEAR 2050.

TOMORROWVILLE
✦ CITY OF THE FUTURE

TRAVELING BY HIGH-SPEED UNDERGROUND TRAIN, you zip toward the city center. As you emerge from the underground train station, you blink in the bright daylight and your surroundings come into focus. What will the urban areas of the future look like?

+ GREEN BUILDINGS

Gardens go vertical, tucked into the walls and roofs of buildings. Food grown close to the people who need it can be picked when it's at its freshest, making for tastier fruits and veggies. And because the food doesn't need to be transported in polluting trucks, it's better for the planet.

+ ROOM FOR WILDLIFE

There's room for people and for animals, too. Future cities will be built with wildlife in mind, with protected areas for native plants and animals.

+ RETHINKING RAINWATER

Not a drop of water that falls from the sky is wasted. Instead of rain gutters, sloped areas of landscaping called bioswales collect and direct water to nourish the city's green spaces.

+ DRONE DELIVERY

It's a bird, it's a plane, it's ... a pizza? Pilot-less drones will flock above urban skies, making deliveries of supplies and food orders and even transporting people from place to place.

+ ALL-WAY ELEVATORS

Going up ... and over, and everywhere in between! One day, elevators that go up and down, side to side, and vertical may be commonplace. They could even change the way skyscrapers are designed—with some elevators appearing outside of buildings, instead of taking up space inside.

+ RECYCLING BY ROBOTS

Never wonder "Is this recyclable?" again. Cities have special waste centers where machines will sort, clean, and recycle everything so materials can be used again and again.

+ WALKWAYS, NOT ROADWAYS

In the future, drones and high-speed transit will mean most people never have to drive. Cities will be designed for pedestrians, swapping roads and parking lots for walking paths and garden areas—and making urban areas more beautiful.

OUT AND ABOUT

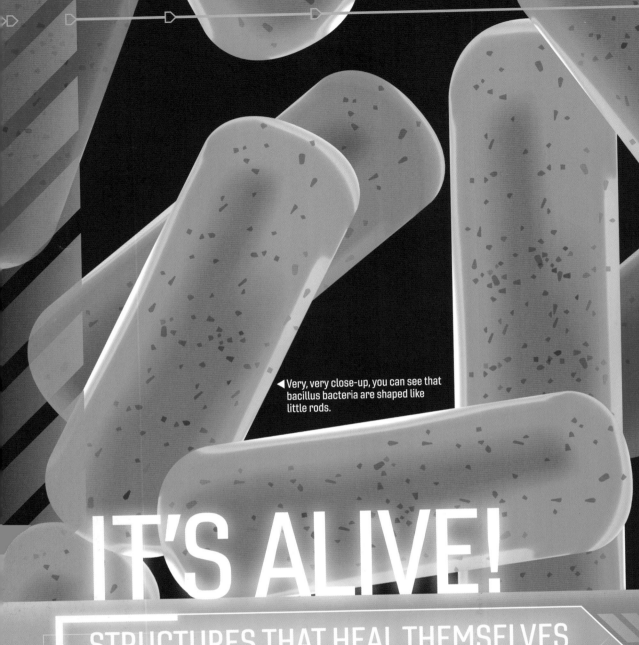

Very, very close-up, you can see that bacillus bacteria are shaped like little rods.

IT'S ALIVE!

STRUCTURES THAT HEAL THEMSELVES

CONCRETE IS ALL AROUND YOU. The world's most popular building material, it fills sidewalks, bridges, and entire buildings. And it's been practically the same for 2,000 years, since the time of ancient Rome. But a new kind of concrete might fill the world of the future: one that can heal itself.

Called bioconcrete, it could be the solution to the major problem with concrete: It cracks. No matter how carefully its materials (water and cement, plus sand, rocks, or gravel) are mixed, all concrete cracks as it ages. When it does, water seeps in, weakening the structure. Eventually, it can collapse.

But bioconcrete is different. It contains not just the three traditional ingredients of concrete but also bacteria and a special kind of salt, calcium lactate. The bacteria, called bacillus, can survive for decades without food or air. They wait, dormant, in the concrete, until a crack forms and water rushes in. The water revives the bacteria, which feed on the salt. Then, the bacteria expel limestone, which closes up the cracks.

Experts say "living" objects made from self-healing materials could one day be common. Cars might repair themselves after a fender bender, wall paint could fix scratches, and roads and bridges could mend themselves after storms.

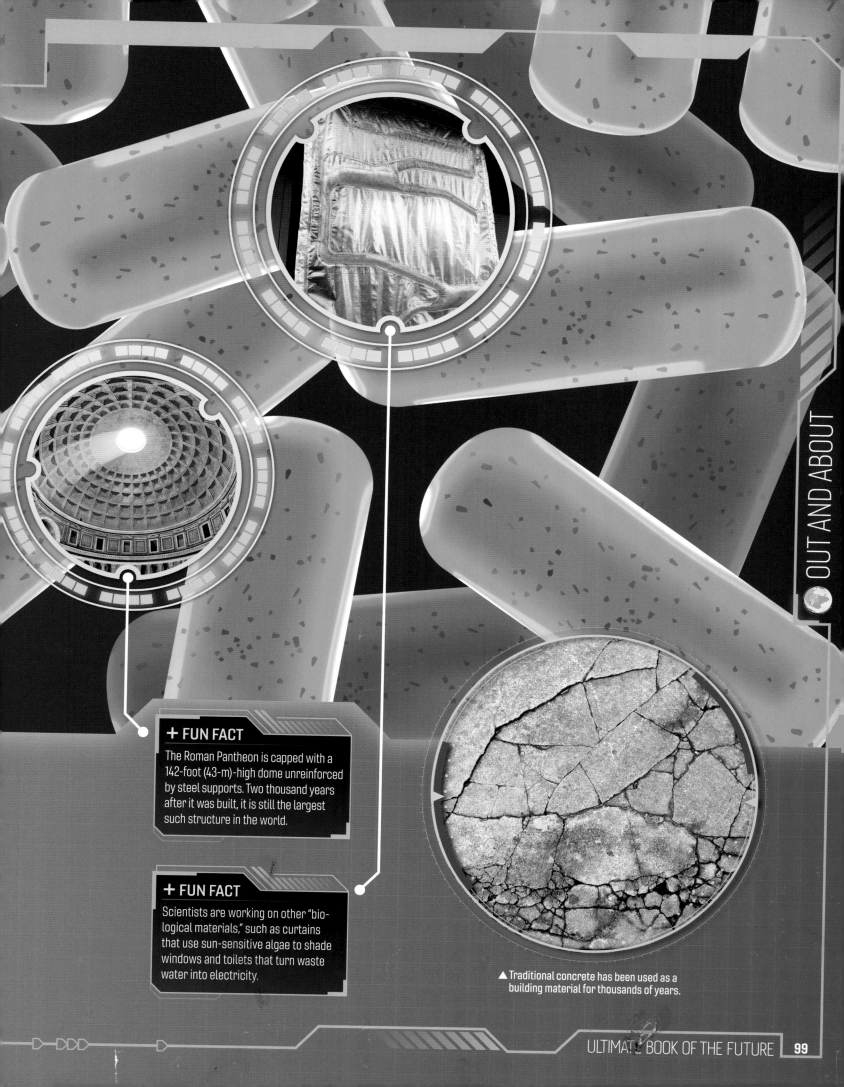

+ FUN FACT

The Roman Pantheon is capped with a 142-foot (43-m)-high dome unreinforced by steel supports. Two thousand years after it was built, it is still the largest such structure in the world.

+ FUN FACT

Scientists are working on other "biological materials," such as curtains that use sun-sensitive algae to shade windows and toilets that turn waste water into electricity.

▲ Traditional concrete has been used as a building material for thousands of years.

FUTURE FOOD
WHAT'S ON THE MENU?

BY 2042, IT'S ESTIMATED THAT THE WORLD'S POPULATION WILL REACH NINE BILLION PEOPLE. THAT'S A LOT OF MOUTHS TO FEED. HERE'S HOW FARMS OF THE FUTURE MIGHT GROW TO MEET THE CHALLENGE.

▶ROBO-GARDENERS

What if robots could take over tough farm tasks like pulling weeds and picking fruit? Engineers are already working on farm bots, like one solar-powered device that searches out weeds in a field and attacks them with precise doses of weed-killer (though in the future, it could use microwaves or lasers instead). Another can judge when strawberries are ready to pick and will pluck just those, leaving the rest to ripen.

◀FORGOTTEN CROPS

Wheat, corn, rice, and soybeans are familiar foods. In fact, they feed two-thirds of the world's population! But what about kedondong, Bambara groundnut, or moringa? These crops have been farmed by humans for centuries, but they remain almost unknown outside of the small areas where they come from. There are about 7,000 of these "lost foods," and some experts are intent on bringing them back to help feed the world's growing population. They say by farming once traditional foods, countries can boost their food supply from within instead of importing wheat, rice, and the rest. Bring on the moringa!

▼ EYES IN THE SKY

Modern farms can be thousands of acres—too large for humans to keep tabs on. But future farmers will get a little help from above, in the form of photos taken from satellites, planes, and drones. They will zip above farmland on a regular schedule to track how crops are growing. Today, agricultural drones can already snap photos at such high resolutions that farmers can zoom in on individual plants.

▲ FLOATING FARMS

As the world's population grows, space for farmland will become scarce—on land. So, some farms will take to the oceans, which cover more than 70 percent of the Earth's surface. The world's first floating farm opened in 2019 off the shore of Rotterdam in the Netherlands. On it, 40 cows are milked by robots to produce 211 gallons (800 L) of milk per day. When the cows aren't on the job, they're free to roam in a green space. That's a roooom with a view!

◀ TEST-TUBE BURGERS

Mmmm. Lots of people love a rich, juicy burger. But today, the beef patty may not come from a cow but be made in a lab. The process starts with a sample of an animal's muscle tissue. From special cells in the tissue called stem cells, scientists can grow new muscle. One tissue sample is enough to make 80,000 burgers! If lab meat becomes mainstream, it could mean enjoying quarter-pounders without harming animals or the environment.

THEN Vs. NOW

▶ROBOT BUTLERS

▶ Even with advanced smart hand dexterity, modern domestic robots are no match for humans.

THEN ▼

WHEN PEOPLE OF THE 1960s imagined the future, there was one thing they knew: Their days of washing dishes and vacuuming floors were numbered. Soon, robots would take over these tasks. Robo-butlers would do it all: Take out the trash, cook dinner, wash the dog. There would be nothing left for humans to do at home but take it easy. Hey, Jeeves, you missed a spot!

▶ In the 1970s, Quasar Industries debuted a robo-butler named Klatu, but the helpful bot turned out to be nothing more than a scam.

TODAY, MANY PEOPLE DO INDEED have household robots. In 2002, a company called iRobot created a robot that could vacuum all by itself—and today, it's sold more than 20 million of the cleaning machines. But robot vacuums can't operate without a human to help out: cleaning the filters, moving cords out of its way, and rescuing the bot after it gets stuck under the couch. Other robots can mow the lawn and clean the pool—but they are far from perfect. And a multipurpose household helper that can follow your commands to bake cupcakes and then walk the dog? Experts say that's still far in the future. So, why the delay? Robots just aren't advanced enough yet. Sure, they can perform complicated tasks—even exploring the surface of Mars! But they almost always need input from human operators. Honda's ASIMO robot can open a thermos and pour the liquid inside into a cup ... but it needs a human to set out the cup and thermos first. FoldiMate, a laundry-folding robot prototype premiered in 2018, can fold a basket full of clothes ... but it needs a person to feed each garment into the machine one by one. With all that setup, you might as well just finish the task yourself!

But maybe the dream of a robot butler isn't dead. In 2021, Samsung debuted Bot Handy, a robotic assistant that the company says can pour you a drink, pick up laundry, load the dishwasher, and set the table. Bot Handy glides around on a tall, thin central body and uses a long arm equipped with cameras to recognize and reach objects. But there's no word on when—or if—Bot Handy will ever be available to buy. For now, we humans are on our own.

OUT AND ABOUT

INTERNET FOR

A CONNECTED WORLD

FOR MANY PEOPLE, the internet is always just a click away. We go online at a whim: to check the day's weather, look up directions, and find out when our favorite shows come on. But for about 60 percent of the world's population, accessing the web is far from simple. About 4.4 billion people currently live without access to the internet. Already, a race has begun to bring internet access to the entire planet, connecting every person living on Earth for the first time in human history.

BIG BALLOONS

In 2020, Google parent company Alphabet sent enormous balloons soaring skyward in Kenya, Africa. But these were no birthday balloons: They were designed to work like mobile cell service towers floating around in Earth's atmosphere. The balloons would transmit internet signals over an area below of about 31,000 square miles (50,000 sq km) that hadn't had reliable service before. Lifted by helium and powered by the sun, the balloons floated 12 miles (20 km) above Earth's surface. They bobbed around twice as high as most airplanes fly.

Alphabet intended to launch a fleet of these balloons around the world that would relay signals from one to another, forming a network that spanned the entire globe. But in 2021, the program shut down, saying the cost of building and launching the balloons was too high. Bringing internet access to the whole world is proving to be a tough challenge.

EVERYONE

SPACE SATELLITES

Rather than balloons riding the waves high up in Earth's atmosphere, why not go even higher—all the way into space? That's what several companies, including SpaceX, have in mind.

SpaceX's project is called Starlink, and it has already begun launching tabletop-size satellites using its Falcon 9 rocket. When the project is completed, which is scheduled for 2027, there should be nearly 12,000 satellites floating above Earth—more than six times the number of all operating satellites in orbit today. The satellites will beam internet data about 50 percent faster than is possible with today's fiber-optic cables, says SpaceX. If successful, the project will bring super high-speed internet to remote areas of Earth, as well as to airplanes, ships, and cars.

WHY WEB?

As the future approaches, humans are becoming more and more dependent on the internet. Most developing technologies, from drones to smart clothing, rely on an internet connection to work. Right now, most people in the developed world have internet access, but in developing nations such as Myanmar and Ethiopia, fewer than two in 100 people can log on. Global internet would allow every person on Earth to access the internet's vast trove of information and use the technologies of tomorrow. A web that's truly worldwide? Sign us on!

+ FUN FACT

Because of the distance between planets, if you did an internet search on Mars, you'd have to wait 30 minutes for the answer to come back to you from Earth.

MADE FROM MUSHROOMS

THERE'S FUNGUS AMONG US

IT'S TIME TO RELAX. YOU SLIDE ON YOUR SLIPPERS, CLICK ON THE LAMP, AND SINK INTO YOUR FAVORITE CHAIR. THERE'S NOTHING UNUSUAL ABOUT THIS SCENE ... EXCEPT ALL OF THESE OBJECTS ARE MADE FROM MUSHROOMS! IT MIGHT SOUND WACKY, BUT MANY SCIENTISTS BELIEVE FUNGI COULD BE THE MIRACLE MATERIAL OF THE FUTURE.

▲FUNGUS 411

Mushrooms, with their stems and caps, are just the part of the fungus we can see above the ground. Most of the organism exists underground, in the form of a network of long, branching, threadlike structures called the mycelium. In 2017, scientists in the Netherlands figured out that they could take a fungus's mycelium and put it into a plastic mold. Then, the fungus will grow to fill the mold, forming anything from vases to lampshades.

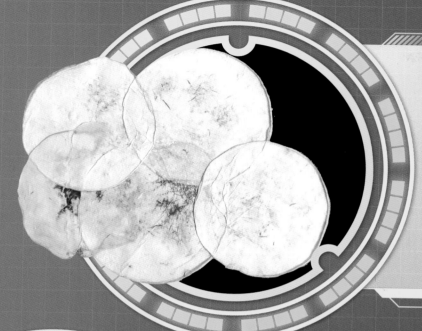

◀ GROWING CLOTHES

Fungus can be shaped into a flexible fabric that resembles leather. That fabric can be cut and sewn into all kinds of clothing, such as dresses and jackets. If wearing a shiitake sweater sounds strange, consider this: The mushroom material resists the growth of microbes—so you can wear it to play sports without getting smelly. And clothing made from fungi is environmentally friendly, too: While making a cotton T-shirt takes 713 gallons (2,699 L) of water, a mushroom garment of the same size uses only three gallons (11 L).

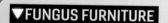

▼ FUNGUS FURNITURE

Fabric made from mushrooms is one thing. But a mushroom material sturdy enough to sit on? That's exactly what two forward-thinking companies unveiled in 2016. They discovered that they could shape mushroom mycelium to grow around a scaffolding of wood chips shaped like a stool base or chair legs. The mycelium ate the wood chips as it grew, and when it ran out, it died and hardened. Treating it with heat and pressure turned it into something strong enough to support a human's weight.

▲ OH GLOW ON

What else can mushroom material do? In 2019, scientists found a way to coat mushrooms with a type of bacteria called cyanobacterium, which produces electricity as it creates food from sunlight. The researchers used a 3D printer to deposit cyanobacteria on a mushroom cap. Then they printed another layer: a pattern of graphene, a material great at conducting electricity. When the scientists shone light on the mushrooms, they generated electricity, which flowed through the graphene pattern, creating an electrical current. The technology is very new, but someday, it could create mushroom material capable of charging a phone or lighting up a room.

THE FUTURE IS NOW

▶REVOLUTIONARY ROBOT

IT HAS TWO ARMS, TWO LEGS AND STANDS ABOUT FIVE FEET (1.5 M) TALL. It can take a walk through the woods, balance on one leg, and land a backflip with ease. But it's not a particularly acrobatic human. It's a robot called Atlas, and it's growing more advanced all the time.

The company that built the bot, Boston Dynamics, wanted to create a human-size and -shaped robot that could operate in a world built for people. That's a big challenge. When Atlas was first unveiled in 2013, it was slow, clumsy, and fell down a lot. By the end of 2014, Atlas could climb stairs, open doors, and drive a car. By 2015, it could operate wirelessly and on battery power. By 2018, it could run over rugged terrain. And now, Atlas can out-perform many humans: A 2018 video shows it hopping over a log and nimbly leaping up a series of uneven wooden platforms. And in 2019, Atlas performed an impressive gymnastics routine, complete with flips.

Boston Dynamics is quiet about the cutting-edge technology that powers its robot. But early versions of Atlas were equipped with two visual systems: one set of cameras that saw the world like human eyes, and a navigation system that worked by shooting out laser beams and analyzing how they reflected off of the robot's surroundings.

Three onboard computers made decisions so Atlas could operate without help from human handlers.

Someday in the near future, robots like Atlas could do all kinds of everyday tasks. They might lift and stack boxes in a factory or enter dangerous areas after natural disasters to survey the damage. That's one break-through bot!

+ FUN FACT

Boston Dynamic's 66-pound (30-kg), dog-shaped bot, SpotMini, can carry half its body weight and run for 90 minutes straight.

+ FUN FACT

When one artificial intelligence expert saw Atlas for the first time, he called it the beginning of a new species, "Robo sapiens."

A08

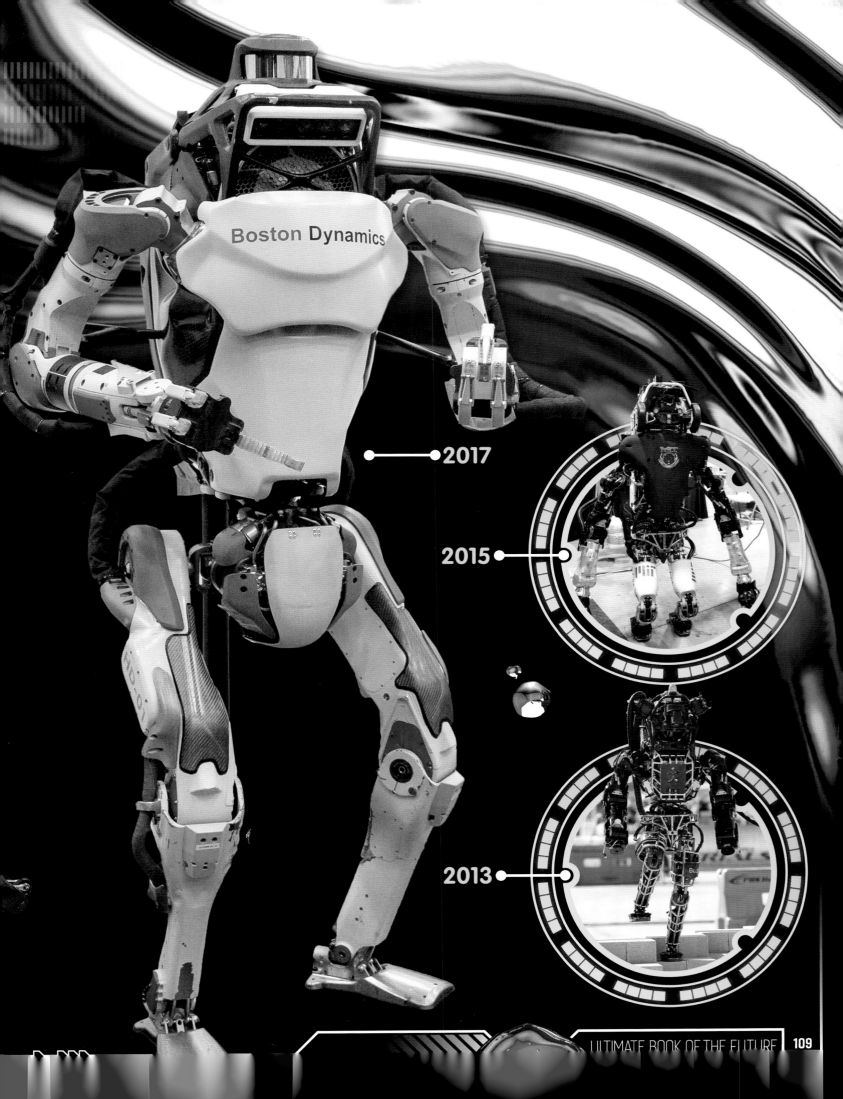

Boston Dynamics

2017

2015

2013

ROBOT-HUMAN COMMUNICATOR

EDUCATION:
BACHELOR'S DEGREE

SKILLS:
ROBOTICS AND CODING | TRAINING IN AI | LANGUAGE AND WRITING

IMAGINE SHOWING UP FOR WORK TO FIND that you're sharing your office not with a human coworker—but with a robot. Right now, robots operate mostly in the background of our lives, vacuuming floors and adjusting the thermostat on command. But in the future, people and robots might team up to work side by side. And someone will need to make sure they get along.

JOB DESCRIPTION

Robot-human teams might work together to care for sick people, perform rescue operations, or run scientific experiments. Humans will handle tasks that require creative thinking and adapting to changing situations—things the human brain excels at. Meanwhile, their robot partners will tackle assignments that people aren't as good at or dislike, such as crunching numbers, doing repetitive tasks, and lifting heavy objects.

But working in a team comes with challenges. What's the best way for people to communicate what they need from their robot partners? And how will robots know when to step in or when to leave things to the humans? That's where you come in. As a robot-human communication specialist, you'll work to program robots to fit seamlessly into a human world and advise human teams about working with bots.

WE OFFER:

 FLEXIBLE SCHEDULE

 WORK WITH ROBOTS

SOUND INTERESTING?

Robot-human communication specialists will need training in artificial intelligence (AI), as well as language and writing skills. In addition to standard school courses, seek out after-school programs in robotics and coding. Later, attend a university with strong AI programs—some already offer specialized classes in human-computer interaction!

APPLY TODAY!

POWERING THE WORLD

THE FUTURE OF ENERGY

TODAY, OIL AND OTHER FOSSIL FUELS, SUCH AS COAL AND GAS, POWER OUR HOMES, RUN OUR CARS, AND PROVIDE ELECTRICITY. BUT BURNING THESE FOSSIL FUELS IS BAD FOR THE ENVIRONMENT, AND EVENTUALLY THEY WILL RUN OUT. IN THE FUTURE, WE'LL HAVE TO TURN TO OTHER SOURCES OF ENERGY. YOU'VE HEARD OF SOLAR AND WIND ENERGY—BUT WHAT ABOUT *THESE* POWERFUL IDEAS?

▶PEOPLE POWER

There are over seven billion people walking around on Earth every day. What if we could harness the power they generate from moving? In 2017, a power-generating walkway opened on London's Bird Street. As pedestrians pass across it, special tiles capture energy from their steps and use it to play recordings of chirping birds and light up displays. That's one smart street!

◀STAR POWER

Every second, the sun gives off more energy than humans have used since the beginning of time. The source of all that power is tiny molecules of hydrogen, fusing together to create helium and spitting out energy as a result—a process called nuclear fusion. Scientists have been trying to harness the power of nuclear fusion on Earth for more than 50 years. Unlike current nuclear fission reactors, nuclear fusion reactors do not produce radioactive waste and cannot suffer a nuclear meltdown accident. Experts say our homes could be fusion-powered before the year 2050.

◄ OCEAN MOTION

Winds can be unpredictable, and the sun can be obscured by clouds. But the ocean's tides are constant. The gravity of the moon and the sun (along with the rotation of the planet) pulls on the water in Earth's oceans, causing coastal waters to rush in and out. Tidal turbines, like a heavy-duty version of wind turbines, can be placed on the seafloor to turn that energy into electricity.

▼ EARTH ENERGY

About 20 times a day, Old Faithful geyser in Yellowstone National Park, U.S.A., erupts, shooting superheated water high into the sky. That water comes from deep within the Earth, where radioactive minerals and leftover conditions from the formation of the planet create intense heat. The steam from hot underground water reserves could be used to turn turbines to generate electricity, producing unlimited power.

▼ WASTE NOT

What if your trash could power your house? That's the idea of a form of power called biomass. Some kinds of waste, such as wood, inedible parts of crop plants, and leftover food, can be burned, releasing energy in the form of heat. Other kinds, such as animal manure and human sewage, can be turned into gas that can be burned for energy. It's poo power!

COULD IT HAPPEN?

►COULD ROBOTS BECOME SMARTER THAN PEOPLE?

MORE THAN 100 YEARS AGO, a psychologist named Edward Thorndike put a cat in a box. The cat paced and meowed until it accidentally hit a lever that sprang the box open. The cat was placed back in the box again and again, and with each try, it took less time to hit the lever. Simply by repeating the task, the cat was learning. Now, scientists are using the same method to create robots that can do something extraordinary: Teach themselves.

GAME ON

In March 2016, an artificial intelligence (AI) program trained using this technique, called reinforcement learning, beat the world grand champion of Go, which is often considered the world's most complicated board game.

That was a big deal for scientists working on artificial intelligence. It's very difficult for a computer to beat a human expert at Go, which has as many possible outcomes as there are stars in the universe. The AI, called AlphaGo, trained by observing thousands of games between human players, noting which moves led to a win. In 2017, a new version of AlphaGo skipped that step and trained by simply playing games against itself until it learned how to beat the game. Like Thorndike's cat, AlphaGo used repetition of a task to teach itself a skill.

BRAIN-BOT CONNECTION

Just because a robot can beat a human at a game doesn't mean it's become smarter than the people who created it. Some experts say that robots will never be as intelligent as humans—that our creativity and intuition will always give us the edge. But others predict that AI will someday be capable of everything the human brain can do, and that robots will be many times smarter than people.

We might need that robo-brainpower. Some researchers estimate that in the future, the world's knowledge will double every 12 hours. How will humans keep up? Some experts think that the answer is electronic implants that will supercharge our brains. These devices could zap pulses of electricity into a part of the brain responsible for a certain skill. Or they might act like an extra storage area, allowing the brain to hold on to extra memories. One problem: It's not clear that this is even possible. But if it was, would you want to use robotics to boost your brainpower?

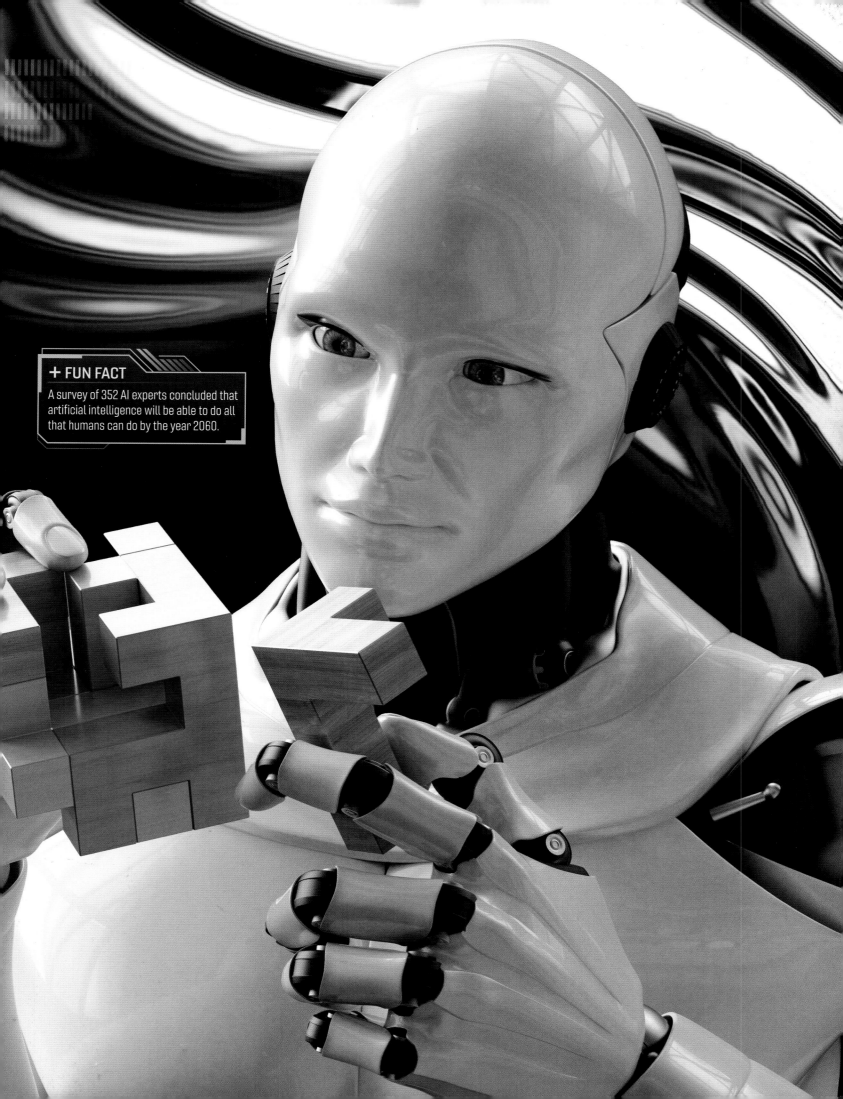

WHEN FUTURISTIC TV FAMILY THE JETSONS felt their stomachs rumbling, they simply pressed a button. Their food-making machine, the Food-a-Rac-a-Cycle, could create a piping hot dish to order in a matter of moments. No dish was too tough to handle, from bacon to banana cream pie. Writers of *The Jetsons* dreamed up this food-in-a-flash system more than 50 years ago. So why are we still waiting on instant meals?

When 3D printers were first introduced in the 1980s, people immediately got excited by the idea of being able to simply print out whatever they were hungry for and eat it on the spot. But the reality of 3D food printing turned out to be a bit disappointing. The printers can only lay down blobs of ingredients in layers—great for things like candies, not so good for much else. A 3D food printer unveiled in 2014, the Foodini, promised to deliver all kinds of savory and sweet dishes made from fresh ingredients. But when users found they had to cook up their own pureed foods to load into the machine first, they were less than thrilled, and the Foodini was never produced. Someday, 3D printers may indeed create the kind of meals we want to eat. For now, instant food is a fail.

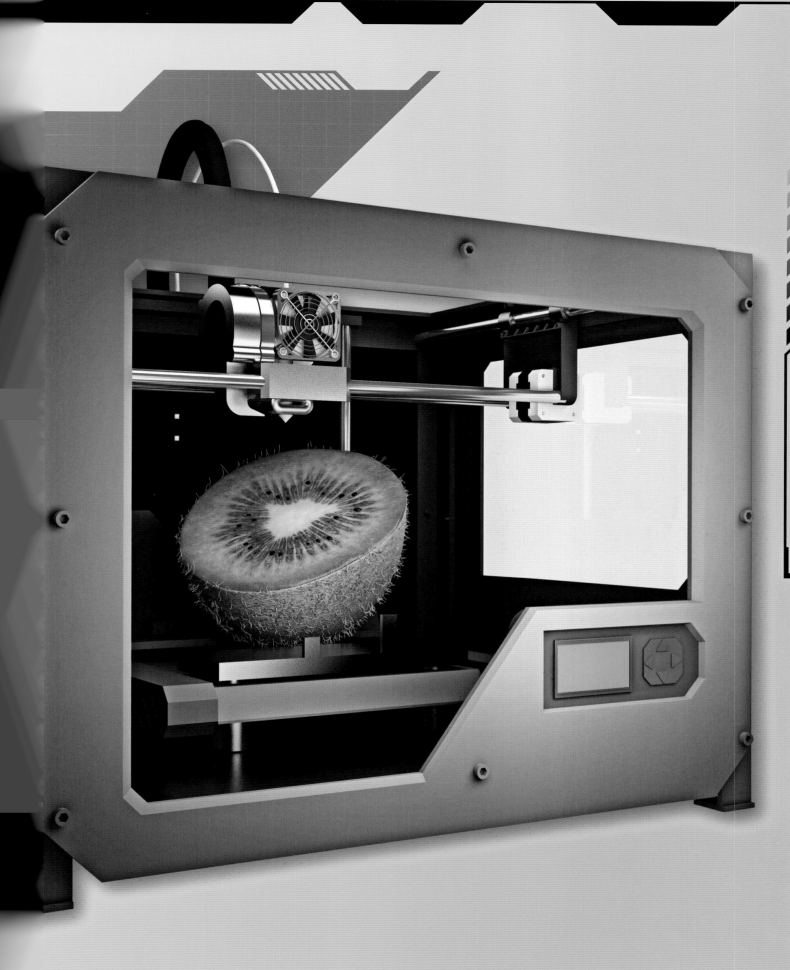

CHAPTER 6 🌍
INSPIRED BY ANIMALS

IMAGINE A FLYING ROBOT AS NIMBLE AS A HUMMINGBIRD, OR A WET SUIT THAT COULD KEEP YOU AS WARM AS AN OTTER IN CHILLY WATER. WELL, IN THE WORLD OF THE FUTURE, THAT MIGHT BE A REALITY! TO CREATE THE NEWEST TECHNOLOGY, SOME SCIENTISTS AND ENGINEERS ARE LOOKING FOR INSPIRATION NOT IN THE LAB— BUT IN NATURE. FROM SPIDER SILK TO A SWARM OF HONEYBEES, SCIENTISTS ARE USING ANIMAL INNOVATIONS TO FIGURE OUT HOW TO MAKE THE CUTTING-EDGE INVENTIONS OF TOMORROW—A SCIENCE CALLED BIOMIMICRY. HERE ARE SOME OF THEIR CREATIONS SURE TO CHANGE THE WORLD.

► This magnification shows spider silk up close and personal.

SILK STRONGER THAN STEEL

SPIDER STUFF

SPIDER SILK IS A MIRACLE MATERIAL. It can stretch up to four times its length and is five times stronger than steel and tougher than Kevlar, which is used to make bulletproof body armor. A human-made mimic of spider silk would be the supermaterial of the future. So it's no surprise that scientists have been trying—and failing—to create spider silk for decades.

But now, researchers at the University of Cambridge in the United Kingdom might have cracked the problem. They've created a material in the lab that is nearly as tough, strong, and stretchy as spider silk. In the future, it could be used to make all kinds of items, from bike helmets to parachutes to airplane wings.

Most manufactured materials, such as nylon, are not simple to make. Chemicals used to produce and dye fabric are often toxic, and processes such as waterproofing create pollution. Spiders, in contrast, use nothing more than water to create the chemical reaction

+ FUN FACT

Spiders have been making silk for 380 million years.

+ FUN FACT

A spider silk–like material could be used to create replacement tendons or as guides to regrow nerves.

that produces their silk. The new artificial material mimics this ability: It's made of a material called hydrogel, which is 98 percent water with fibers of silica and cellulose floating inside. The researchers found that when the water evaporates, a superstrong thread is left behind.

Spider silk's sturdy quality comes from its ability to absorb a lot of energy. That keeps the web from breaking when a bird or insect flies through it. The new material has the same property, which makes it perfect for protective clothing for police officers and helmets for athletes. The material can also be absorbed by the human body, so it could be used for stitches that disappear after the wound is healed. That's some incredible arachnid power!

COULD IT HAPPEN?

►COULD WOOLLY MAMMOTHS COME BACK TO LIFE?

TEN THOUSAND YEARS AGO, woolly mammoths roamed the Earth. These enormous mammals were around 13 feet (4 m) tall and weighed about six tons (5.44 t). And of course, they were covered with thick coats of brown fur that kept them warm in their Arctic environment. Woolly mammoths shared their home with another species: ancient humans. Could we someday walk the planet together again?

SUPER SPECIMENS

Woolly mammoths lived in what is now Siberia and the northern part of Canada. When they died, their bodies were often preserved in the snow and ice. Starting around the 1700s, people began discovering the remains of these ancient beasts. Some are in incredibly good condition: One preserved mammoth discovered in 2013, nicknamed Buttercup, had most of her body, part of her head, and her trunk intact—and when researchers began to remove the body, they noticed dark blood oozing.

If these animals' blood can survive, can their DNA survive too? Many scientists around the world are obsessed with the idea of finding mammoth DNA in one of these ancient specimens and using it to bring these woolly wonders back to life.

A MAMMOTH PUZZLE

It won't be easy. DNA, the body's genetic material that carries all the information about how a living thing will look and function, begins to break down very quickly after death. In 2019, scientists in Japan extracted nuclei—the compartments of cells that contain DNA—from a mammoth discovered in 2010 in Russia. They transplanted those nuclei into mouse eggs, hoping the cells would come back to life. They didn't. But the cells did show some activity—a sign that the researchers might be on the right track.

Scientists might not need DNA from mammoths at all. George Church, a genetics expert at Harvard University in Cambridge, Massachusetts, U.S.A., is working on a different way of bringing the prehistoric giant back from extinction: adding the genetic adaptations of mammoths, such as genes for long fur, to the DNA of Asian elephants. The hybrid DNA could someday be used to grow a full-size, living mammoth.

Would you want to bring mammoths back to life?

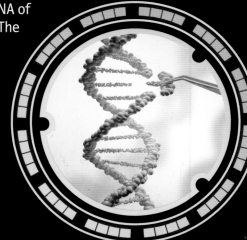

OTTERLY WATERPROOF

A WET SUIT WITH FUR

SEA OTTERS LOVE TO TAKE IT EASY. The mammals can often be spotted floating on their backs, relaxing in the water between meals. They sure look comfortable—and they manage to stay that way even in waters that are 61°F (6°C) or colder! Otters' ability to keep warm and toasty even in chilly water made engineers wonder: Could they mimic the mammal to create a future wet suit that would allow divers to explore the coldest waters?

Unlike many other sea-dwelling mammals, such as seals and whales, otters don't have a layer of insulating fat under their skin to help their bodies hold in heat. Instead, they rely completely on their fur. Otters have the world's thickest fur, with as many as one million hairs per square inch (6.5 sq cm). For comparison, you have about 100,000 hairs on your entire head! The fur is so dense that it traps a layer of air next to the otter's body, which keeps cold water from touching their skin.

+ FUN FACT

Typical wet suits are made of neoprene, a type of rubber. They trap a layer of water against the wearer's skin, which is warmed by body heat.

+ FUN FACT

Sea otters' paws don't have dense fur to keep them dry, so the animals often hold their paws up above the surface of the water when they're resting. Hands in the air!

A group of engineers at the Massachusetts Institute of Technology in Cambridge, Massachusetts, created a material modeled after the animal's fur. They used lasers to blast hundreds of holes in a mold. Then, they filled the mold with silicone, creating a sheet covered with hairlike projections. Finally, they tested how well the material repelled water by dunking it into a container of water. They discovered that the more closely packed the silicone "hairs" were, the better the material repelled water—just like an otter's coat!

One day, a similar material could be used to create water-repellent fabric perfect for wet suits. In the future, human divers could stay as warm in the water as otters.

ANIMAL CONSERVATION TECHNOLOGIST

EDUCATION:
SCIENCE   ECOLOGY

SKILLS AND QUALIFICATIONS:
TRAINING IN AI

IT'S THE MIDDLE OF THE NIGHT IN CHAD, AFRICA. Armed with guns, machetes, and spears, a group of poachers walks through the savanna. They're on the hunt for black rhinos.

Poaching is illegal, but it's still a major problem in many places around the world. Black rhinos, African elephants, tigers, and sea turtles are just a few of the creatures threatened by poaching. Today, stopping poachers is extremely difficult. But in the future, conservationists—people who protect wildlife—will have new tools to put an end to illegal hunting.

JOB DESCRIPTION

Eighty percent of poaching happens at night, when hunters can hide under the cover of darkness. Couple that with the environment—millions of square miles of wilderness—and catching poachers in the act is no easy feat. But conservationists have already begun outsmarting poachers using technologies of the future: drones and artificial intelligence (AI).

WE OFFER:

 WORK WITH ANIMALS

 TRAVEL

The conservationists of the coming decades will work with local government officials to target a group of poachers. First, undercover police officers will learn about an upcoming poaching operation and alert conservation organizations. Then, the drones fly in. Artificial intelligence—designed by an expert—watches the footage, using knowledge of how local animals typically move through the area to find evidence of poacher activity. Infrared cameras will use heat to map an area, allowing the drones to locate poachers even when they're hiding in a forest or tall grass. Game over.

SOUND INTERESTING?

Conservationists of the future will need to understand how and why animals become endangered. They'll also need training in artificial intelligence to program drones to seek and find poachers. Start by studying science with a focus on ecology—the science of how organisms relate to each other and their environment.

+ FUN FACT

AI cameras that can identify humans and animals were installed at Serengeti National Park in Tanzania in 2019 to help stop elephant poachers.

SWARM!

A FLOCK OF BOTS

A GROUP OF BUZZING DOTS APPEARS IN THE SKY. Together, they turn and dip, moving through the air in such harmony they are more like one mega-creature than a group of individuals. Is it a flock of birds or a colony of bees? Neither: It's a swarm of robots.

Scientists have long been fascinated by the synchronized group movements of creatures like ants, bees, termites, and schools of fish, a behavior called swarming. Someday in the near future, they hope to tap into this phenomenon to create robots that can work together to complete all kinds of tasks.

SWARM SCIENCE

The way swarms work is strange and mysterious. While groups of humans often organize themselves by following a leader, swarming organisms operate in a totally different way: There is no one individual in charge. Creatures in a swarm don't follow directions from a leader—instead, each independently responds to its environment. Somehow, they can all work together this way, accomplishing a group goal like moving an object many times larger than they are. And by using the power of teamwork, they have a kind of smarts far greater than the brainpower of critters operating alone.

Researchers say that this phenomenon, called swarm intelligence, can be used to explain all kinds of events. From the way blood cells organize to form a clot to how cars on a highway create patterns, many groups display the same behaviors that organize a school of fish or flock of birds. Understanding swarm intelligence can help experts solve problems, such as figuring out how to help wounds heal or predicting how traffic will flow in order to design better roads.

BAND OF BOTS

What if scientists programmed a group of robots to behave like a natural swarm? Kilobot, designed by a team at Harvard University in 2010, is barely bigger than a quarter and each one costs just about $15 to make. Each individual kilobot can only do a few things: detect its neighbors, measure distance, move across a flat surface, and flash a light. But when working together, they can arrange themselves into shapes like a letter K or a star—without specific instructions from a human to tell them how.

In 2016, researchers at Stanford University took swarm robotics to the next level. They developed 1.1-inch (29-mm) robots designed to work together like ants. When just six of the mini bots moved in tandem, they could perform an impressive feat—moving a full-size car!

GROUP PROJECT

Scientists are excited about the future of swarming robots. Swarms of robots could totally reshape factories, replacing legions of individual, specialized machines with a single team of bots that can work together to accomplish different tasks, building something from start to finish at record speed. Flying swarms could pollinate a field of crops. And all-terrain swarms could march into dangerous areas to stack sandbags before a hurricane or contain toxic chemical spills. Now that's what we call teamwork!

▲ These swimming robots, called Blueswarm, can synchronize their movements just like a school of fish.

HUMMINGBOT

THIS BIRD CAN FLY

ZZZZZIP! In a blur of wings, the fast flier whizzes by. This aerial acrobat is so talented that it can hover in place, something only a handful of birds on Earth are capable of. But this isn't a real-life hummingbird: It's a robot! If all goes well, you might see similar bots zipping all over the place in the future.

The hummingbot is the invention of a team of scientists at Purdue University in West Lafayette, Indiana, U.S.A. The researchers spent several summers in Montana, where they studied how hummingbirds fly. Back in the lab, they used 3D printers to create the robot's body and added carbon-fiber wings. The finished bot weighs just .42 ounce (12 grams), making it about the same size as a common species called Rivoli's hummingbird.

Most birds fly by flapping their wings up and down, getting the upward force of lift only on the downward flap. But hummingbirds are unique. They rotate their wing bones as they beat their wings, tracing a horizontal figure eight in the air. That motion creates lift on both the upward and downward flaps, giving

▲ Purdue's hummingbird robots use machine learning to fly like real hummingbirds do.

+ FUN FACT

3D printers work by placing layers of a material on top of each other to create an object.

the bird a power boost that allows it to hover. Hummingbirds can also shape-shift their wings, making tiny changes in the way they hold their feathers to alter their wing structure, an ability that allows them to switch direction in an instant.

The researchers mimicked this unique flying ability in their robot. The hummingbot can change its wing direction more than 30 times a second to outfly even the most agile of drones. Right now, the bot can only soar while tethered to a power source, but its creators hope that soon, it will be battery-powered, able to zoom and dive through the sky just like the real thing. The creators believe that someday, bots like this could be used for searching disaster areas, filming, and military investigation.

HARD-HEADED

CRITTER-INSPIRED HELMETS

TAP. TAP. TAPTAPTAPTAP! THAT'S THE SOUND OF A WOODPECKER BANGING ITS BEAK AGAINST A TREE TRUNK. IF WE HUMANS COPIED THE BEHAVIOR, WE'D WALK AWAY WITH A POUNDING HEADACHE—OR WORSE! BUT WOODPECKERS—AND MANY OTHER CREATURES BESIDES—HAVE SPECIAL ADAPTATIONS THAT KEEP THEIR BRAINS FROM BEING BRUISED DURING THEIR HEAD-BANGING ACTIVITIES. SCIENTISTS ARE TAKING NOTE.

▼HELMET HOG

Hedgehogs spend their days climbing trees, getting as high as 30 feet (9.1 m) as they search for insects to munch on. But they're not the most agile of animals—they often fall out of their high perches. That sounds scary, but like pangolins, hedgehogs are able to roll their bodies into a ball, with their sharp spines pointed out. The spines absorb the impact, and the hedgehog unrolls and walks away without injury. Researchers at the University of Akron in Ohio, U.S.A., are attempting to copy the hedgehog's method of protection by designing a liner for helmets made of material that mimic's the hedgehog's spines. They hope their helmet will be ready for action within a few years.

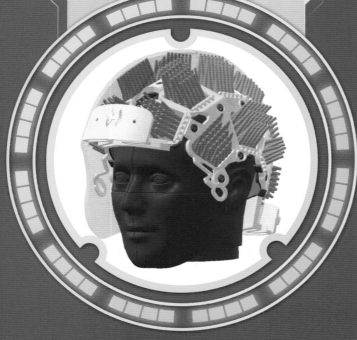

►SCALY SECRETS

The pangolin is one of nature's strangest animals. It almost looks like a living artichoke, the result of the scales that cover its body. Those scales aren't for show—when a pangolin is threatened, it curls up into a ball, concealing its soft underbelly. Its scales are so tough that even a lion can't bite through them! That behavior gave a group of inventors an idea for a helmet that could fold back on itself, forming a collar around the neck when not in use. While traditional helmets are bulky, the retractable helmet is easy to transport and wear on the go. Its creators hope that before too long, their idea will become a real product.

◄SHELL SHOCK

You might have held a conch shell to your ear on the beach to hear the sound of the ocean. But you probably didn't know that you had in your hands one of the toughest materials in the sea. Though it's composed of about 95 percent calcium carbonate, the same material as brittle chalk, conch shells are a thousand times tougher. They get their strength from their unique structure, composed of three layers, which makes it difficult for cracks to spread and grow. In 2017, researchers at the Massachusetts Institute of Technology made a replica of the material in their lab. In the future, it could be used to create better helmets, as well as body armor.

►BIRD BRAIN

When high school football player Berto Garcia got a concussion on the field, he was told he couldn't play any longer. So he decided to look to nature for a solution, by finding out how woodpeckers are able to take repeated blows without suffering ill effects. Among other adaptations, he found, the birds have special muscles in their necks that help hold their heads steady. Garcia created a football helmet that attached to a uniform's shoulder pads on either side, holding the player's head steady even if they got slammed by on opponent. The device is still in the testing phase, but someday, it could help athletes protect their noggins on the field.

THE FUTURE IS NOW

▶ PLASTIC-EATING BACTERIA

PLASTIC IS A BIG PROBLEM. Every day all around the world, people put their groceries in plastic bags, sip out of plastic straws, open plastic packaging ... and then toss it all in the trash. Experts estimate that humans have produced about 9.1 billion tons (8.3 billion t) of plastic—the weight of 25,000 Empire State Buildings. Around 79 percent has ended up in landfills. There, it will take hundreds or even thousands of years to break down ... if it ever does. But what if nature could speed the process along?

In 2016, a strange bacterium was discovered in a Japanese waste dump. Surrounded by plastic trash for generations, it had evolved the ability to eat a molecule called polyethylene terephthalate (PET) commonly used in plastic bottles. Things get even weirder: While experimenting with the bacterium to figure out how it does its plastic-digesting trick, scientists accidentally created a new, mutant form of the bacterium that had an even bigger appetite for trash. The molecule responsible, PETase, can break down PET in just a few days—a process that normally takes about 450 years! The scientists hope that within the next 10 years, their discovery could be used to change the way plastic recycling is done.

A bacteria-based recycling system could break down PET bottles into their molecular parts. Then, brand-new bottles could be created from those building blocks, making it possible to reuse the same plastic over and over again with zero waste. Nature, the scientists say, might already be creating its own solution to the plastic problem. We just need to give it a boost.

THE VERY HUNGRY WAXWORM

Another plastic-eating critter was discovered in 2017—also by accident! When biologist and amateur beekeeper Federica Bertocchini noticed waxworms—common pests that eat beeswax—on her beehives, she removed them and put them in a plastic bag. When she came back later, the worms had escaped and the bags were full of holes. They had eaten their way out! Further research showed the worms can break down plastic in just hours. Bertocchini hopes that if her team can discover how the worm's body does this, they could mimic the mechanism to help eat up the world's plastic.

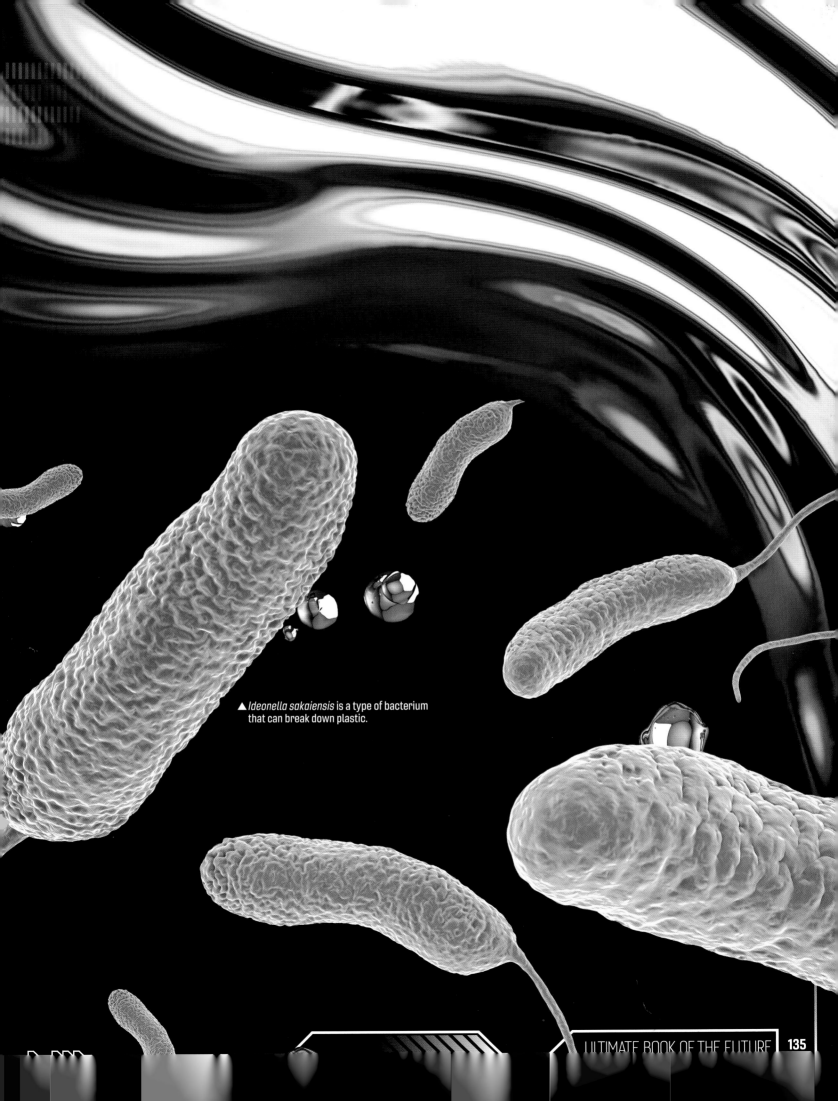

▲ *Ideonella sakaiensis* is a type of bacterium that can break down plastic.

SHARK SENSOR

UNDERSEA SENSE-ATION

SHARKS ARE SOME OF NATURE'S MOST LETHAL HUNTERS. But they don't just use their senses of sight, hearing, and smell to seek out a tasty meal. They have a special, extra sense: the ability to detect electricity. Now, scientists have adapted this ability into a futuristic material capable of detecting even the faintest electrical signals underwater.

All living creatures emit electrical fields, but they are so weak that they are very hard for most creatures to detect. But sharks, along with some other ocean predators such as rays, have special organs called ampullae (AM-puh-lay) of Lorenzini. They look like a line of small holes near the shark's mouth. When electrically charged particles floating in the water enter the holes, special cells detect their presence, alerting the shark that

something living is swimming nearby. This sense is so sensitive that sharks can use it to find fish even when they are hiding under the sand at the bottom of the sea.

Inspired by the shark's sense, a group of scientists at Purdue University in Indiana set out to create a material that could sense electricity the way a shark does. They used a substance called samarium nickelate, which has strange properties experts don't totally understand yet. But they do know that its properties can

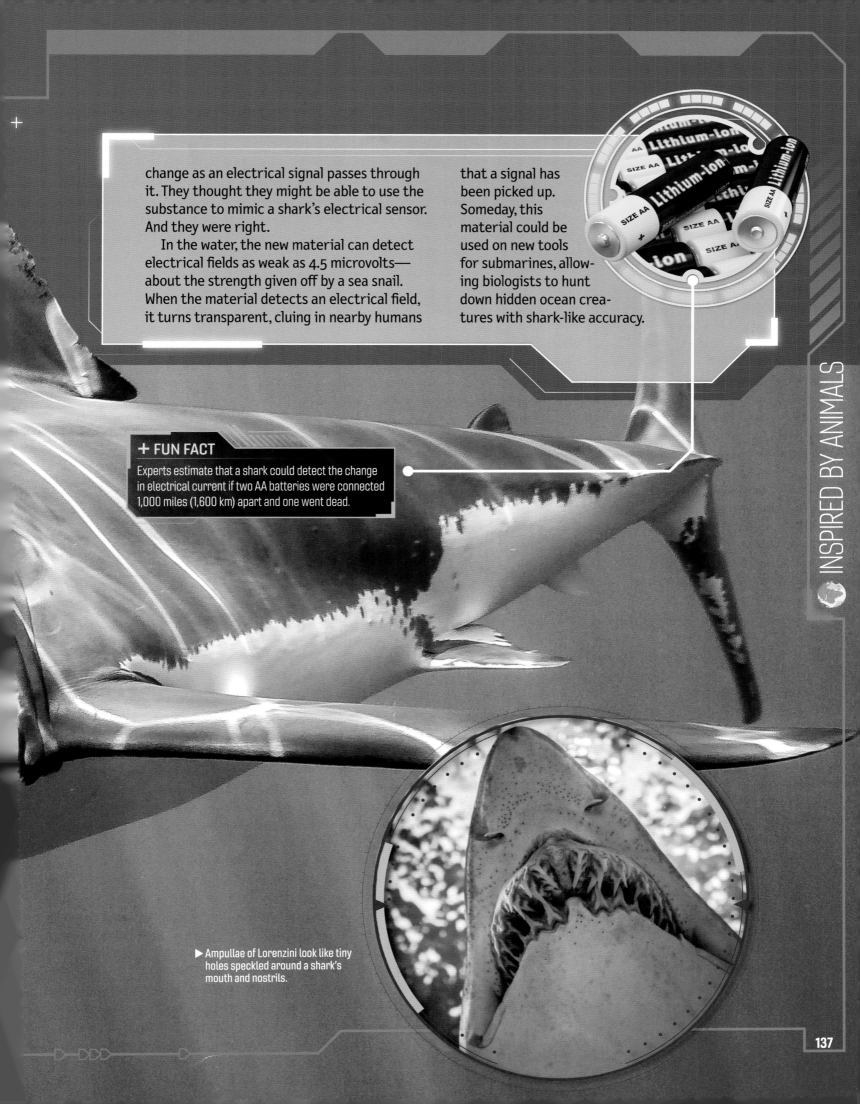

change as an electrical signal passes through it. They thought they might be able to use the substance to mimic a shark's electrical sensor. And they were right.

In the water, the new material can detect electrical fields as weak as 4.5 microvolts—about the strength given off by a sea snail. When the material detects an electrical field, it turns transparent, cluing in nearby humans that a signal has been picked up. Someday, this material could be used on new tools for submarines, allowing biologists to hunt down hidden ocean creatures with shark-like accuracy.

+ FUN FACT

Experts estimate that a shark could detect the change in electrical current if two AA batteries were connected 1,000 miles (1,600 km) apart and one went dead.

▶ Ampullae of Lorenzini look like tiny holes speckled around a shark's mouth and nostrils.

FUTURE FAIL

SHRINK RAYS

WHEN THE SUPERHERO ANT-MAN is ready to shrink, he presses a button on his supersuit. In an instant, he's the size of the insect he's named for. In this tiny form, he can sneak just about anywhere. Shrinking stuff on demand would be a neat trick indeed. But in reality, experts say this sci-fi superpower will never come to be.

The laws of physics make shrinking impossible. Everything on Earth is made of atoms, with a central nucleus orbited by particles called electrons. There is a great distance between the two: If you magnified an atom of hydrogen's nucleus so that it was the size of a basketball, then the electron that whizzes around it would be two miles (3.2 km) away. That's a lot of empty space! But alas, the properties of atoms mean a nucleus and its electrons simply can't be squeezed tighter together. And even if it was possible to squash atoms to shrink something, the result would be an incredibly dense object: If Ant-Man's atoms were squeezed to make him teeny, he would be so heavy for his size that he would sink straight through the Earth. That's no way to fight crime.

FAIL

CHAPTER 7

BUILDING BETTER BODIES

A HUNDRED YEARS AGO, THERE WERE NO ANTIBIOTICS. THERE WERE NO VACCINES TO PREVENT MANY DEADLY DISEASES, SUCH AS TUBERCULOSIS OR YELLOW FEVER. WE DIDN'T KNOW ABOUT DNA AND COULDN'T SCAN THE BRAIN. HEALTH AND MEDICINE HAVE COME FAR SINCE THEN. AND IF THE EXPERTS ARE RIGHT, THE NEXT 100 YEARS WILL HOLD EVEN MORE ASTOUNDING ADVANCEMENTS. HUMANS MIGHT SOON REPLACE LOST LIMBS WITH BIONIC BODY PARTS THAT WORK BETTER THAN THE ORIGINALS, CURE DISEASES WITH MEDICINES DISCOVERED AT THE BOTTOM OF THE SEA, AND EVEN—MAYBE—LIVE FOREVER.

NO MORE NEEDLES

OUCHLESS VACCINES

MORE THAN 200 YEARS AGO, an English country doctor named Edward Jenner administered the world's first vaccine. It began a new era of medicine: Soon, diseases that had once killed or harmed millions, such as smallpox and polio, were nearly wiped out. But as every kid who's been poked with a needle at the doctor's office knows, getting vaccinated is no fun.

But what if scientists could re-engineer vaccines to take away the ouch? Right now, experts around the world are developing vaccine patches that are stuck on the arm and deliver the medication through tiny needles less than a millimeter long. Someday soon, getting a shot might be as easy as slapping on a Band-Aid.

So far, early studies have shown that the vaccine patch seems to work as well as a traditional shot. That's good news for anyone with a fear of needles. But it's also promising for people in developing countries. In many parts of the world, medical professionals have to travel long distances to vaccinate kids in need, carrying coolers to keep their supplies from going bad. In contrast, the vaccine patch doesn't need to be refrigerated, and it's so simple to use that people can do it themselves.

The vaccine patch is just one new needle-free technology. Other researchers are working on vaccines that can be inhaled or dissolved on the tongue. Nasal vaccines, which work by spraying a mist of virus-fighting ingredients up the nose, are already available to treat some diseases. One company is even developing a new syringe modeled after the mouthparts of a mosquito, which often draw blood without the person even noticing. One thing's for sure—all these options sound better than getting the flu!

◄ Edward Jenner gives a child a vaccine.

▲ Close-up and magnified, these spikes might look scary, but they're actually tiny!

BIONIC BODIES
◆ CYBORG SCIENCE

JOHNNY MATHENY IS TEACHING HIMSELF HOW TO PLAY THE PIANO. It's an impressive accomplishment—especially considering Matheny's left arm is robotic. Some call Matheny a cyborg: After losing his arm to cancer in 2017, he became the first person in history to live with a sophisticated carbon fiber replacement that he can control with his mind. And get this: The newest generation of bionics are so sophisticated, some are superior to the biological body parts they're replacing.

+ SPEED RACER

The Flex-Foot Cheetah is a prosthetic so innovative that it's been worn in Olympic competition. It's so advanced, in fact, that experts debate whether Cheetah-wearing athletes have an unfair advantage over those with biological legs.

+ LOUD AND CLEAR

The newest hearing aids don't just turn up the volume: They can block out surrounding noise and focus on a conversation, create soothing white noise, and even act as a phone.

+ LEG UP

Sensors on the PowerFoot BiOm robotic leg take in 250 data points at each step. They can sense when the user is walking up a slope or crossing uneven terrain, then replicate the motions a human foot and leg would make. People have even used the leg for rock climbing.

+ EXTREME EYES

These bionic peepers use a chip implanted onto a sightless person's own eyes that converts light into electrical impulses, then feeds them to the brain—just like a biological eye does. One test patient outfitted with the chip could read a clock and see letters.

+ SENSE-ITIVE

The fingertips on the newest robotic arms can detect texture, pressure, and temperature and send signals back to the user's brain, giving the robotic fingers the sense of touch, just like real ones.

+ ARMED AND READY

The Modular Prosthetic Limb has 17 built-in motors, allowing it to bend and twist in ways that a human arm can't match.

TEST-TUBE ORGANS

REPLACEMENT PARTS

WHEN AN OCTOPUS LOSES AN ARM, it's no big deal. The creature's body begins to regrow the limb, from its inner nerves to its outer suckers, until it has a replacement just as good as the original. Unfortunately, the same isn't true for humans: We can't regenerate damaged body parts … for now, that is. Scientists are now learning how to grow organs in labs. Soon, they believe, new organs will be made to order.

NEW LOOK

Traditionally, the only option for a person with a failing heart or kidney has been organ transplantation. In this process, the body parts are taken from a human donor and surgically placed into the patient who needs them. But transplantation has problems. There aren't enough donor organs to go around: For example, only about 2,000 hearts are available each year, not nearly enough for the 50,000 to 100,000 people who need one. And even when a patient in need is lucky enough to receive a donor organ, his or her body often targets the replacement as something that doesn't belong, then attacks and destroys it, something called organ rejection.

But what if the new organ didn't have to come from another person? What if it could be made of the person's own cells? That's the idea behind lab-grown organs. Since about 2006, people have been walking around with artificial parts such as bladders and windpipes. To make them, researchers first scan the patient's body to determine the exact size and shape of the organ that needs replacing. Then, they build a scaffold—a framework that the new tissue can grow on—out of a substance that naturally occurs in the body called collagen. Finally, they add cells from the patient and put the whole thing in a special environment with plenty of food and oxygen to help the cells grow. Over a few weeks, the cells grow around the scaffold until they form the new organ. That organ is then surgically implanted into the patient.

▼ 3D-printed artificial bladders already exist.

PRINT ON DEMAND

Windpipes and bladders are simple structures. But scientists think that soon, they'll be able to create all kinds of body parts. Some say that something like a lab-grown lung could be less than 10 years away.

In fact, in 2018, a team of scientists in the U.S. at the University of Texas Medical Branch in Galveston made a big step when they used cells from pigs to grow lungs in a lab and then successfully transplanted them into the animals. Months later, the pig lungs were still working perfectly. In 2019, an international team of scientists grew replica human blood vessels for the first time. When transplanted into mice, the blood vessels connected to the animals' circulatory system and sprouted a network of smaller vessels.

Creating complex organs such as kidneys is tricky because they are made up of many different types of cells arranged in a particular order. To build them, scientists are experimenting with using 3D printing. In 2016, scientists at the National Museum of Health and Medicine in Silver Spring, Maryland, U.S.A., used a special 3D printer to create ear, bone, and muscle tissue. Replacement hearts and kidneys could be next. In the future, a lost limb may be no problem. Like an octopus, we'll simply regrow it.

THEN VS. NOW

►MEDICAL SCANNER

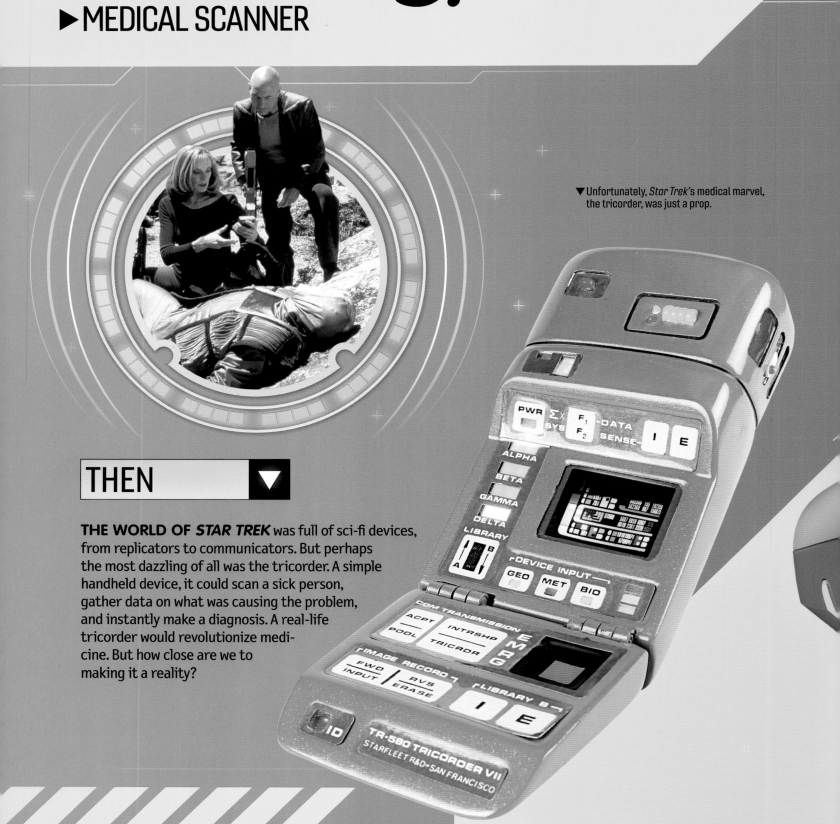

▼ Unfortunately, *Star Trek*'s medical marvel, the tricorder, was just a prop.

THEN ▼

THE WORLD OF *STAR TREK* was full of sci-fi devices, from replicators to communicators. But perhaps the most dazzling of all was the tricorder. A simple handheld device, it could scan a sick person, gather data on what was causing the problem, and instantly make a diagnosis. A real-life tricorder would revolutionize medicine. But how close are we to making it a reality?

IN 2011, the XPRIZE Foundation announced a world-wide competition calling inventors to develop one. And in 2017, a winner was announced: a working prototype invented by an emergency room physician from Philadelphia, Pennsylvania, U.S.A., named Basil Harris. The device is just a prototype, and it needs to be tested before it's available for regular consumers to use. But just like the *Star Trek* version, it can make a diagnosis in minutes and is simple enough for anyone to use.

Called DxtER, it doesn't look like the *Star Trek* tricorder: Instead of a single handheld piece, it's a kit of items that includes a small digital stethoscope, a heart monitor that sticks to the chest, a spirometer that a patient blows into to measure lung health, and a finger probe that can note levels of glucose, white blood cells, and other substances in the blood. All the devices are connected to an app, which explains how to use the sensors.

DxtER can diagnose more than 30 common conditions including pneumonia and diabetes. Experts think the device could change the future of medical care. In rural places where people may not have easy access to doctors and hospitals, DxtER could catch medical problems that might have gone untreated. And for people with chronic illnesses who have trouble getting to the doctor, DxtER could help them monitor their health from home. Experts say this is one piece of science fiction tech that's about to become a fact of the future.

BUILDING BETTER BODIES

▲ The DxtER kit contains tools that can be used to diagnose more than 30 common conditions.

▶ A man demonstrates how to use DxtER to monitor health and diagnose illnesses.

BASIL LEAF

► COULD HUMANS LIVE FOREVER?

IN THE MEDITERRANEAN SEA floats one of the planet's most extraordinary creatures. A pale pink disk, it doesn't look like much, but this jellyfish, called *Turritopsis dohrnii,* has a survival skill like none other: When injured or dying, it can return to its juvenile form, becoming young again. That ability gives *Turritopsis dohrnii* its nickname: the immortal jellyfish. Scientists are studying these creatures closely, hoping to uncover secrets about human aging. Is it possible that someday, we could go on living far into the future?

AGE GAP

Some scientists believe that within the next few decades, it could be possible for humans to live 1,000 years or more. Normally, as time passes, our cells undergo changes: Our DNA mutates, cells stop dividing, and harmful junk—by-products of cellular activity—builds up. All these processes together cause us to age. But experts such as Cambridge University researcher Aubrey de Grey think that we will soon be able to use advanced medicine to keep these changes from happening, and stop the aging process in its tracks. Many other scientists disagree, saying that we know far too little about how aging works to tell whether it can be stopped. But some people think we may know enough in the future, possibly centuries from now. That belief is why some people have gone so far as to freeze their bodies in liquid nitrogen in the hopes that someday, humans will have the

▲ Some people hope that if they freeze their bodies—in a facility like the one shown above—they can one day be brought back to life.

scientific knowledge to bring them back to life— for good. One company charges $200,000 to preserve and store a body. But experts point out that there's no evidence that it's even possible to revive someone who has been frozen. And as people from philosophers to vampire novelists have long wondered—even if it's possible to live forever, is it a good idea?

MIND THE MACHINE

No matter how advanced technology gets, it might be impossible for our bodies to go on forever. Some researchers believe there is a limit on how long it's physically possible to live: perhaps 125 years. But what if we don't need our bodies at all? Some people, including famed futurist Ray Kurzweil, believe that by 2045, we might become immortal by uploading our brains into computers. Then, we could leave our bodies behind and live forever as machines.

To do it, we'd have to map the wiring of the whole human brain—a task we're nowhere near accomplishing with current technology. And it's a mystery whether transferring the inner workings of a brain into a computer would also transfer the person's feelings, thoughts, and personality, too. But that's not stopping some futurists from trying.

Would you want to live forever?

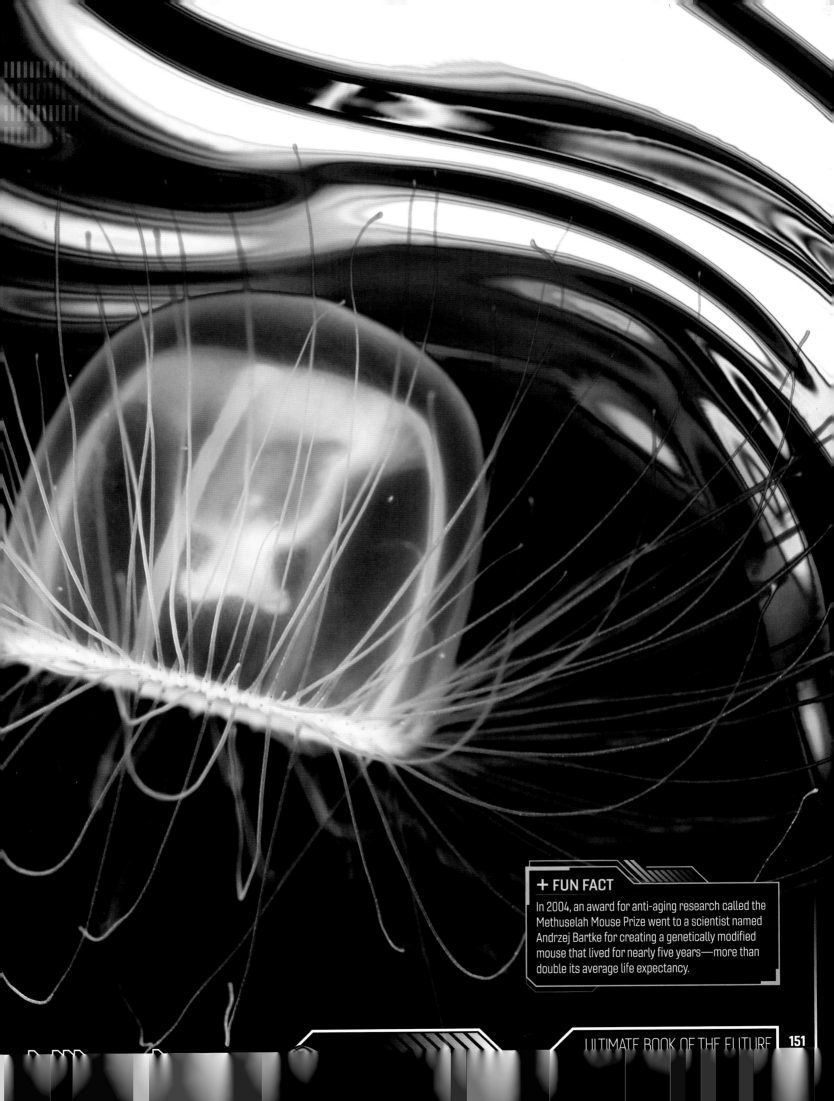

WACKY MEDICAL TECH

HEALTH CARE GETS CREATIVE

OUCHLESS VACCINES AND ORGANS GROWN IN LABS MIGHT SEEM HARD ENOUGH TO BELIEVE. BUT *THESE* MEDICAL TECHNOLOGIES ARE EVEN STRANGER: FROM PAINT THAT KILLS MICROBES TO BANDAGES THAT ZAP THEIR WEARERS, THESE ARE SOME OF THE HARDEST-TO-BELIEVE—BUT 100 PERCENT REAL—HEALTH INNOVATIONS IN DEVELOPMENT.

▶ SMART PILLS

Scientists have long been working to develop digital "pills." Once swallowed, they'd be able to track gut health, deliver medicine to just the right spot, or even take pictures using a tiny camera. One obstacle: the batteries used to power these pills, which can be unsafe when they degrade. So engineers at the Massachusetts Institute of Technology developed a new kind of battery powered by the patient's own stomach acid. Now that's a pill that's easy to swallow!

◀ ELECTROCUTING BANDAGES

A bandage that zaps you sounds like it would hurt—not heal. But scientists have known for decades that electricity can help the body repair wounds faster, by helping skin cells to grow, for example. And now, researchers at the University of Wisconsin-Madison, U.S.A., have developed a prototype bandage that delivers mild electrical pulses into the skin. The device is powered by body movements, meaning no bulky batteries required.

◄ MEDICAL MAGGOTS

They're creepy, they're crawly, they feed on dead flesh—and they can be used to treat wounds. It might sound repulsive, but studies have found that putting special, disinfected maggots on injured areas can be more effective than the usual treatments. That's because maggots eat dead flesh while leaving healthy tissue untouched—meaning they can precisely clean wounds and prevent infection. The treatment isn't popular, but it's catching on—and in the future, it could be commonplace.

▼ BRAIN CELLS MADE FROM PEE

In China, researchers have managed to figure out a way to get brain cells, or neurons, from human urine. Urine contains skin cells that are shed from the lining of the kidneys and flushed out of the body. The researchers collected these cells, then tweaked their genetic code to transform them into neurons. Someday, this new technique could provide a simple way to study brain diseases such as Alzheimer's. So it's not "waste" after all!

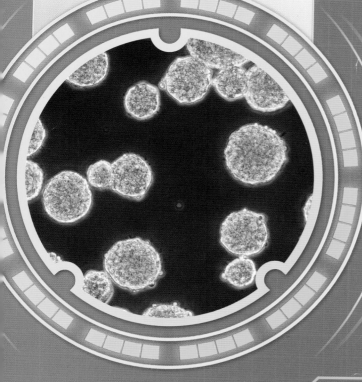

▲ GERM-KILLING PAINT

"Superbugs" are microbes that frequently infect hospitals and can't be killed by traditional antibiotics. They cause more than 35,000 deaths every year in the United States, and the risk is rising. But what if the hospital itself could fight back? Researchers in South Dakota, U.S.A., are developing a new paint containing a substance that can kill many microbes, including antibiotic resistant strains. Someday, it could cover the walls of hospitals, schools, and other public places.

UNDERSEA MEDICAL RESEARCHER

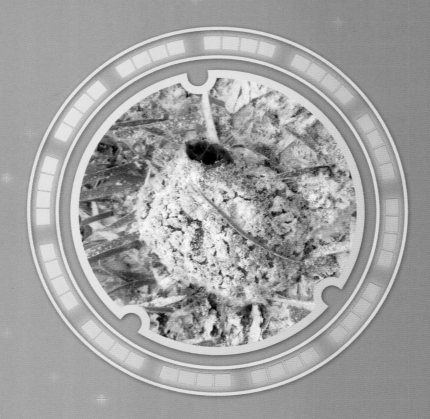

EDUCATION:
BIOCHEMISTRY | MARINE BIOLOGY

SKILLS:
SCUBA DIVING

***TECTITETHYA CRYPTA* DOESN'T LOOK LIKE MUCH.** This blob-like sea sponge sits at the bottom of the ocean in warm Caribbean waters, usually covered with sediment. But hiding inside this unlikely creature are two chemicals that have been used to develop multiple medicines, including one that became the first ever drug to treat leukemia, a form of cancer. It was the first approved cancer drug to ever come from the sea. But experts think it will be far from the last.

The ocean holds some of the last unexplored places on Earth. All kinds of unusual chemicals are hiding there—and scientists think some hold the secrets to curing deadly diseases. In the future, medical researchers will swap lab coats for wet suits and dive in search of new medicines.

JOB DESCRIPTION

Many drugs have their origins in nature. Half of the top 10 most commonly prescribed medications in the United States come from animals, plants, or microorganisms, including treatments for high blood pressure, diabetes, and arthritis. But the oceans—which hold 99 percent of the livable space on this planet—are a place we have hardly even begun to look.

WE OFFER:

 ADVENTURE

 ON-THE-JOB TRAINING

Already, scientists from all over the world are searching the seas to find new chemicals that could be useful to humans. They don scuba gear and plunge into the water to collect samples of marine organisms like algae, sponges, sea urchins, and corals. Over the past 30 years, scientists have already extracted more than 20,000 new substances from creatures like these, and some are currently undergoing scientific testing to see if they could make good medicines. In the future, researchers will dive even deeper into the world of marine medicine, visiting largely unexplored places such as deep-sea vents with the mission of saving lives on the surface.

SOUND INTERESTING?

Marine medical researchers will need a background in biochemistry, a field that involves concepts from both biology and chemistry. They will also need an understanding of marine biology to know how and where to focus their search. And of course, they'll need an adventurous spirit to take the plunge!

☑ COOL SCUBA GEAR

APPLY TODAY!

CUTTING EDGE

TRAINING DOCTORS WITH VIRTUAL REALITY

IT'S A FEW DAYS BEFORE A DOCTOR IS scheduled to perform a life-saving brain surgery. The brain's complex folds and ridges make it extremely complicated to operate on—and a slip could cost the patient his ability to talk, breathe, or remember. The surgeon wants to prepare. But instead of picking up a scalpel, she grabs a pair of virtual reality goggles.

Hospitals and medical schools around the world are already using virtual reality technology to help train doctors. Medical students can

learn about the body's respiratory system by inspecting a 3D hologram of a lung. Or they can digitally shrink down to miniature size and step inside a virtual heart to see its valves first-hand. And doctors-in-training can virtually practice procedures such as fixing a broken bone before they try it out on flesh-and-blood patients.

Virtual technology is proving to make a real difference. One study found that students who used headsets to study human anatomy—such

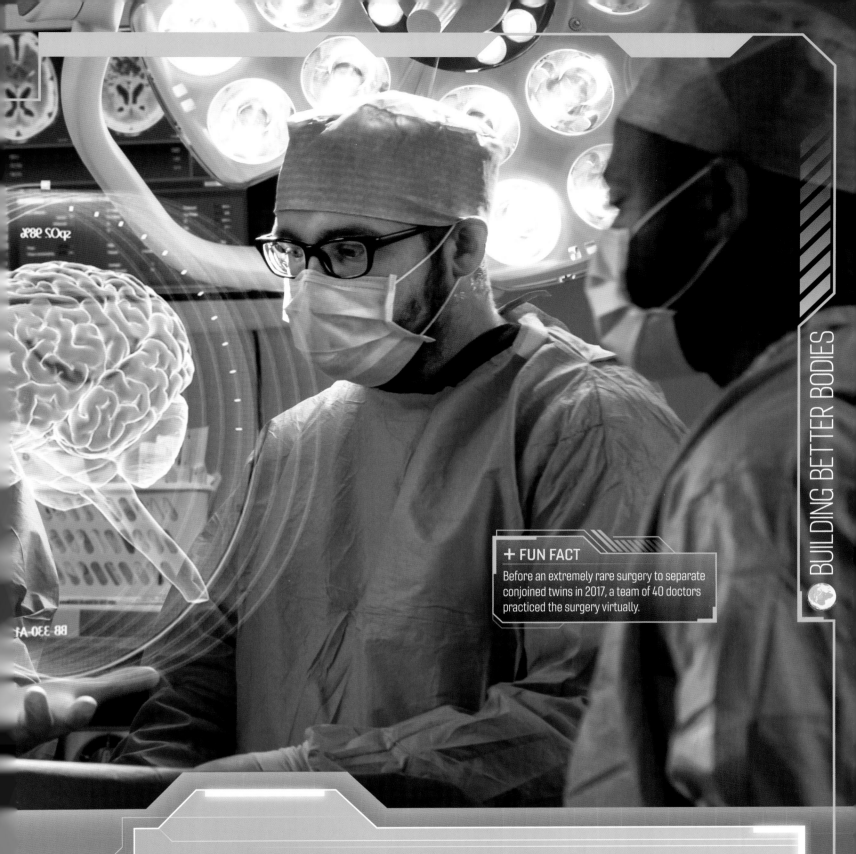

+ FUN FACT

Before an extremely rare surgery to separate conjoined twins in 2017, a team of 40 doctors practiced the surgery virtually.

as how the bones, muscles, and blood vessels of the arm work together—learned the information twice as fast as students who studied the traditional way.

And virtual reality isn't just for doctors. Patients are using it, too: Some are playing games that help them regain movement after surgery. Others are watching digital versions of their own surgeries before they happen so that they understand what they're about to experience. Talk about modern medicine!

FUTURE FAIL.

INSTANT HEALING ▼

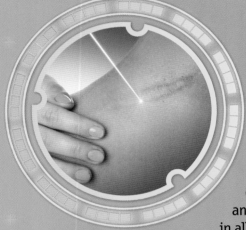

▲ Today, doctors can use lasers to make scars less visible.

OH, NO! You're repairing a broken part on your spacecraft when your tool slips and cuts your arm. You hurry to the ship's doctor, who inspects your wound, then picks up a small device. She aims it at your cut, presses a button, and the device shoots out a beam of high-powered energy. As you watch, your skin closes, healing the cut instantly. Now, you can go right back to work, instead of getting stitches and waiting weeks to heal. These medical ray guns appear in all kinds of science fiction, most famously in *Star Trek*. So why don't we have them in real life?

Humans come with built-in self-healing technology. When your skin gets cut, your body springs into action. Special blood cells stick together like glue at the wound, forming a clot that dries and turns into a scab. The scab protects the cut by keeping germs out, while underneath, new skin grows, knitting the edges of the cut together. People can heal from injuries as severe as broken bones and damaged organs. But our bodies take time to repair. In 2015, doctors reported that they had discovered a way to speed up the process: By aiming ultrasonic waves at injured skin, they found they could stimulate body cells to heal quickly. But the technology only shortens the process by 30 percent. Pretty cool, but very far from the instant healing of the sci-fi ray gun.

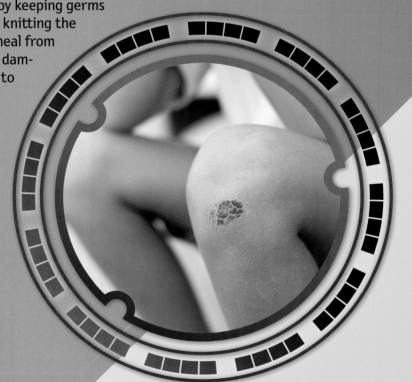

▲ The humble scab is just one of many ways the human body has to heal itself.

◄ *Star Trek* character Leonard McCoy was the chief medical officer aboard the U.S.S. *Enterprise,* with a host of high-tech tools for healing.

CHAPTER 8 🌍
FUTURE FUN

YOU MIGHT USE YOUR FREE TIME TO RIDE A SKATEBOARD OR VISIT A THEME PARK. FAST-FORWARD TO THE FUTURE, AND THAT SKATEBOARD MIGHT HOVER ABOVE THE GROUND. AND THAT THEME PARK MIGHT BE FILLED WITH REAL-LIFE DINOSAURS! THE TECHNOLOGY OF TOMORROW WON'T JUST HELP US LIVE BETTER AND WORK SMARTER, IT WILL ALSO BE A WHOLE LOT OF FUN. FROM INVISIBILITY CLOAKS TO ROBOT ART, HERE'S A PEEK INTO THE ENTERTAINMENT OF THE FUTURE.

THEN VS. NOW

►HOVERBOARDS

◄ Marty McFly catches some air in the '80s film *Back to the Future II*.

THEN ▼

AUDIENCES WATCHING THE 1989 sci-fi flick *Back to the Future II* were thrilled when hero Marty McFly jumped on a hoverboard to evade a pack of bad guys. Flying across roads and waterways, bouncing off buildings and car windshields, Marty made a dramatic escape. The year? 2015. Now, we're past that date, and we're still not riding hoverboards. But we might not have to wait much longer: Some companies say real-life hoverboards are floating on the horizon.

▲ This hot pink hoverboard is just a prop, but today real hoverboards are in the works.

▼ The Lexus Slide hoverboard

IN 2014, an internet video caused a sensation when it showed legendary skateboarder Tony Hawk swooping on a different kind of board: a hoverboard. California tech company Hendo designed a board that uses magnets to levitate riders about six inches (15 cm) above the ground. Then, the next year, car company Lexus introduced an even slicker-looking hoverboard: the Slide. With a sleek carbon-fiber body, it appears to float an inch or two (2.5–5 cm) above the ground in a teaser video.

Now for the bad news: The Hendo's battery lasts for only a few minutes, and the board was so difficult to maneuver that even Tony Hawk only hung on for a few spins. Both boards rely on magnetic levitation to get airborne—and since magnets must have other magnets to repel against, the boards need a special magnetic track below in order to hover. That means riders couldn't zoom over sidewalks and turf. But future hoverparks could be embedded with magnets or steel to give hoverboarders the ride of a lifetime ... no running from bad guys required.

FUTURE FUN

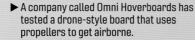

▶ A company called Omni Hoverboards has tested a drone-style board that uses propellers to get airborne.

BOT-TICELLI

ROBOT ARTISTS GET CREATIVE

GREAT ART MAKES US FEEL SOMETHING.
Standing in front of a painting by Picasso or a sculpture by Michelangelo can make us feel calm, sad, awed, or many other emotions. But it's not possible that a machine could ever create art that moves us ... or is it?

Some people think so. Andrew Conru is the founder of Robot Art, a competition involving artwork created by robots. Roboticists and computer engineers submit paintings, and then a panel of art critics and voters from the public judge the art. In past years, some of the pieces were created by humans using robotic technology, such as robot arms that the humans direct. Other pieces were totally original, created by artificial intelligence with no input from humans.

Conru says that robotic artwork isn't as far-fetched as it might seem. Artists follow "rules" to create perspective (the illusion of three dimensions), decide where shadows should fall, and paint humans and animals

+ FUN FACT

In 2018, auction house Christie's sold a piece of AI-generated art for $432,500.

with the correct proportions, plus much more. Conru thinks that robots can be trained to follow these rules, too, and make masterpieces just as good as a human's.

Soon, Conru believes, robot artists will be skilled enough to fool viewers into believing their art was created by a human. In 2018, artist Mario Klingemann trained an AI by inputting thousands of European oil portraits

from before 1900. Then, the AI tried to mimic what it had seen. Some of the results look strange, while others are more convincing. But will a robot's paintings ever give us the same reaction as the work of a great human artist? Only the future will tell.

◄ With the help
of augmented
reality, fans can
become Pokémon
trainers in the
real world.

CHANGING YOUR VIEW

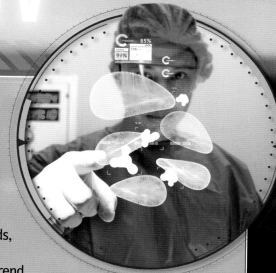

▼ Augmented reality could help surgeons practice their techniques.

AUGMENTED REALITY

IN 2016, people holding out their mobile phones ran across parks and crossed streets in cities around the world. They were playing Pokémon Go, a game that uses mobile devices to show players a world of colorful monster-like characters hopping and hiding on their local streets. More than 100 million people joined the craze to capture virtual creatures.

Pokémon Go is an example of augmented reality, a type of technology that adds computer-generated information—such as sounds, text, or adorable fantasy critters—to the real-world environment. Many experts believe augmented reality will be the next big tech trend.

A NEW REALITY

You might not realize it, but augmented reality is already a part of your everyday experience. Televised football games show the first-down line as a yellow line that moves across the field through the course of the game. Social media apps allow you to digitally alter your face, showing what you'd look like with puppy ears or as an adorable baby. Many interior design stores have apps that allow the user to take a photo of their living room and then virtually try out couches, chairs, and paint colors to find the perfect fit.

Augmented reality is already beginning a new era of games. In one, you color in the characters in a paper coloring book. Then, on a phone or tablet, you can launch an app that uses the device's camera to analyze your design, then virtually re-create it as a 3D character on the screen. In another new game, the surface of the moon is superimposed onto the user's real surroundings. The users can step into the augmented reality to explore the lunar environment, just as astronauts did for real on the Apollo 11 mission.

TECH WATCH

By the year 2025, experts estimate that the augmented and virtual reality industry will be worth over $25 billion. They predict that within 10 years, many people will be walking around with augmented reality devices such as "smart-glasses" that add virtual details to the environment—giving directions, telling us where the nearest coffee shops are, and more.

The augmented reality technology of tomorrow could help people explore the world without leaving their own houses, even visiting places like Mars and the Great Barrier Reef. Doctors could use it to practice surgeries without experimenting on real flesh and blood. It could help out with everyday tasks such as repairing plumbing or fixing a car, by lighting up parts and drawing virtual arrows to show what to do.

From gaming to medicine, augmented reality is already changing the way we use devices to interact with our world. And once we can truly meld imagination and reality, the future is full of possibilities.

HIDE-AND-SEEK

INVISIBILITY CLOAK

HAVE YOU EVER WISHED for a real-life invisibility cloak? With a swish of fabric, you become the world's greatest spy, watch any sporting event from the front row, and of course, play tricks on your friends. And you may not need to be a wizard to get one: Scientists are getting closer to making this magical piece of clothing a reality.

Here's the basic science behind the idea: Our eyes detect an object when light reflects off the object's surface and bounces back to our eyes. But if the path of the light is bent in just the right way, it could make that object seem to disappear.

That notion powers an invention currently in development by a team of Canadian scientists. In 2019, they announced a patent for a material that has layers of special lenses embedded in it. When light hits these lenses, it is bent in such a way that an object covered by the material isn't visible, but what's behind it is. This creates the illusion of invisibility.

This technology is far from capable of making a human being disappear. It only works in one direction, meaning an observer has to be standing in just the right spot for the object to disappear. But this technology could be an important step. In the future, the concept could power a real-life invisibility cloak—no magic required.

▶ Don't worry—cloaking devices won't make you actually invisible. At least, not yet.

◀ In 2019, a toy company unveiled a cloak modeled after the one worn by actors in the Harry Potter movies: It works like a green screen and uses an app to allow the wearer to "disappear" in photos and videos.

FUTURE FUN

COULD IT HAPPEN?

▶ COULD JURASSIC PARK COME TRUE?

IN THE *JURASSIC PARK* FILMS, hapless humans run from real-life monsters: enormous *T. Rex* and packs of vicious velociraptors with gnashing teeth and tearing talons. Of course, these animals have been extinct for millions of years. But is it possible that, like in the movies, we could really bring them back to life someday? And what would a real Jurassic Park be like to visit?

FROM DNA TO DINO

In *Jurassic Park*, scientists re-create dinos using dinosaur DNA they find in blood sucked up by an ancient mosquito preserved in amber. Scientists say they do sometimes find biting insects preserved inside amber, or fossilized tree sap. But when insects become encased in amber, their blood isn't preserved, just their hard outer bodies—so this method most likely wouldn't work in real life.

But there might be other ways for scientists to get their hands on dino blood. In 2015, researchers examined fossilized bones from Cretaceous-era dinosaurs and found what they think are fragments of blood cells. There was no DNA, however, which breaks down quickly when exposed to sunlight and water. In fact, the oldest DNA discovered so far is less than a million years old, and dino DNA would have had to survive for much longer—at least 66 million years. So using DNA to re-create the dinosaurs is probably impossible. But scientists keep looking, just in case.

FEATHERED AND FLASHY

If future scientists do somehow solve the problem of how to bring dinosaurs back, where would we put them? Paleontologist Jack Horner, the science adviser for all the *Jurassic Park* films, has a few ideas. Unlike in the films, a dinosaur park wouldn't need tall fences and superstrong gates. Instead, dinosaurs could probably live on protected areas of land, much like where elephants and lions now live in Africa, says Horner. Many dinosaurs were peaceful plant-eaters, and watching them in the wild probably wouldn't be too different from hanging out with a herd of antelope. Of course, some, like velociraptors, were hunters—but like lions on the Serengeti, they would be unlikely to attack humans.

And those dinosaurs would likely look very different from their movie versions. Scientists once thought that dinosaurs were covered in scales. But they now know that many species were probably covered in feathers—just like their descendants, modern-day birds. And some scientists think these dinos were not dull green and brown, but fantastically colorful. In 2010, scientists found evidence that a kind of dinosaur called *Sinosauropteryx* sported a tail ringed in bands of orange and white feathers. That's nothing like the movie monsters!

Would you want to bring extinct dinosaurs back to life?

◀ Today, scientists believe that some species of dinosaurs would have actually had feathers rather than scales.

WHEEEE!
◆ FUTURE THEME PARK

DO YOU LOVE WHIZZING THROUGH THE SKY ON A ROLLER COASTER? Then put your hands in the air for the theme parks of the future!

House of Horrors

+ FRIGHT FACTOR

Today, creepy rides usually appear around Halloween and then disappear for the rest of the year. That makes sense: If visitors were able to experience them over and over again, they wouldn't be nearly so scary. But in the future, rides will use face recognition to identify individual visitors and change the experience each time—so people never see the same ghost twice. Boo!

+ NO MORE LINES

High-speed rides are thrilling. Waiting in long lines to get on? Not so much. Luckily, some theme park experts think lines will soon be a thing of the past. Using their mobile devices, visitors will be able to book a ride in advance. You'll show up at the pre-determined time and walk right on.

+ A WHOLE NEW WORLD

Some theme parks won't have rides at all. Instead, they'll be like video games brought to life, where visitors will walk through the gates and into a totally new world. They'll chat with fairies, play games with trolls, and go on quests.

+ SCREEN TIME

Traditional theme parks send cars filled with visitors past crowds of singing animatronic animals or pirates. But experts say the theme parks of the future will mix physical experiences, like animatronic characters and special water and fire effects, with virtual visuals. Headsets will put visitors in the middle of an intergalactic battle or steps away from attacking zombies.

+ GAME ON

The theme parks of tomorrow will make the experience similar to playing a game. Visitors might earn points by driving a go-kart over an image on the floor or finding a hidden object. Roller-coaster riders could stop, slow, or turn their car with their voices or gestures. Sounds like a wild ride!

THE FUTURE IS NOW

▶ HOLOGRAPHIC PERFORMANCES

HATSUNE MIKU IS 16 YEARS OLD AND WEARS HER HAIR IN LONG TURQUOISE PIGTAILS. As one of Japan's biggest pop stars, she has performed for sold-out crowds and opened for celebrity acts like Lady Gaga. But Miku isn't real—she's a hologram.

Miku's creators didn't intend for her to become a superstar. They created her as an avatar to go along with their song-creating software. When users wrote songs with the program, Miku would sing them on the screen. She quickly took on a life of her own, and now, there are thousands of fan-created Miku songs online. The most popular ones become part of her live shows, where the virtual star is projected onto a screen onstage.

Most pop stars can't directly interact with their fans. But Miku is different. Her songs—she has more than 100,000 of them—have been written by her followers, many of them people who have never made music before. Her fans create her choreography and direct her music videos. That has made Miku a huge star: One of her songs even became Japan's most popular karaoke song.

Miku's success has led some people to predict that the future might hold more holographic pop stars than human ones. After all, Miku may not be real—but her legions of screaming fans are.

ENCORE

Wish you could see Elvis in concert? Soon, you may be able to. Hologram technology is already bringing back popular performers of the past, from rock-and-roll legend Buddy Holly to pop idol Michael Jackson to rapper Tupac Shakur. Specialists study tapes of old shows and carefully craft choreography, which a live actor performs wearing a motion-capture suit. Then, tiny details like the angle of a singer's hand on the microphone or the beads of sweat on his brow are added. The whole process can take months to get just right. What do you think: Are performances from the past cool or creepy?

▶ Hatsune Miku performs
at a packed concert.

BRAIN BEATS

MAKING MUSIC WITH YOUR MIND

IN 2016, a Seattle, Washington, U.S.A., audience was treated to a musical performance like nothing ever before. The musician, a neurologist and amateur jazz musician named Thomas Deuel, sat motionless in a chair, a cap studded with electrodes over his head. As one musician played the drums and another strummed the base, Deuel was playing an instrument, too: his brain.

Deuel is the inventor of a device called the encephalophone (en-SEF-ah-lo-fone) that can read a person's brain waves and turn them into sounds. The device uses EEG, or electroencephalogram, technology, which records the electrical activity within the brain's motor cortex, the section responsible for moving our arms and legs. When the musician hooked up to the machine thinks about extending a finger or moving a leg up and down, those thoughts move notes up and down a scale. The EEG signals are transmitted to a computer, which turns them into

+ FUN FACT

New research suggests that playing a musical instrument rewires the brain so that it can complete complex tasks more easily.

+ FUN FACT

You might like pop while your grandpa likes oldies—but studies show no matter what kind of music it is, the same brain area is triggered in everyone when they listen to their favorite tunes.

the sounds of a piano, violin, or other instruments.

Deuel thinks musicians could use the encephalophone to create brand-new tunes. He also thinks the technology could help people with neurological conditions such as a spinal cord injury. Many of these patients have muscles that no longer respond to brain signals, but motor cortexes that are undamaged. By teaching them to play the encephalophone, Deuel believes he may be able to help their brains connect to their bodies once again. What a sound idea!

COOL BOTS

ROBOTS ON THE MOVE

PREDICTING THE FUTURE ISN'T EASY. WILL WE HAVE FLYING CARS, GIANT SOLAR SHIELDS, OR CLOTHING MADE OF MUSHROOMS? WE CAN'T BE SURE. BUT THERE'S ONE THING EXPERTS ARE CERTAIN THE FUTURE WILL HOLD: A WHOLE LOT OF ROBOTS. HERE ARE SOME OF THE BEST BOTS IN DEVELOPMENT.

▲ BIRD BOOST

Penguins don't fly ... or do they? Robotics company Festo's AirPenguin floats gracefully through the sky, like a metallic, penguin-shaped blimp. Its head, tail, and wings all move, and the bot can shift to fly forward or backward. It's just one of many animal-inspired robots created by Festo, which include an enormous flying jellyfish and a robotic elephant trunk.

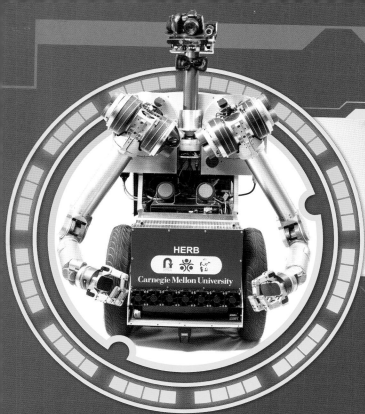

◄ COOKIE BOT

Separating the filling from a cookie sandwich without breaking it can be challenging for a human, let alone a robot with metal fingers and no sense of its own strength. That's why HERB (Home Exploring Research Butler) went viral when the bot did just that on camera. HERB can also unload a dishwasher and microwave a meal. Not bad.

► JUMP AROUND

What happens when an exploring robot finds itself with a wall between it and where it wants to go? If it's the Sand Flea robot from Boston Dynamics, it jumps. Using carbon dioxide–powered pistons, the tiny 10-pound (4.5-kg) bot can leap up to 33 feet (10 m) straight in the air, then repeat the feat up to 30 times before needing a recharge. Sand Flea can jump with such precision that it can land right inside a second-story window, then send back video of what it discovers inside.

◄ SWORD PLAY

Master swordsman Isao Machii can slice the top off of a piece of fruit or cut a bamboo pole into slivers. And Motoman MH24 can match him move for move. This bot has extremely dexterous humanoid arms that enable it to do that and much more. Motoman can build a camera, catch and cook a fish, and play the drums. It can even dance!

FUTURE

ANTIGRAVITY

IN THE 1971 FILM *Willy Wonka and the Chocolate Factory*, Charlie and Grandpa Joe take a taste of candy mastermind Willy Wonka's Fizzy Lifting Drink ... and float right up to the ceiling! Science fiction has featured antigravity technology since the 1600s. And it's no wonder—a device that could cancel out the effects of gravity would revolutionize space travel, dramatically reducing the amount of energy it takes for a spacecraft to escape the pull of Earth. Not to mention it would be a lot of fun to float! So where are the antigravity machines?

In 1992, a Russian physicist named Evgeny Podkletnov announced that he had made a major discovery: He had successfully tested a device able to shield an object from gravity. The scientific community was incredibly excited. NASA spent seven years and hundreds of thousands of dollars trying to build a device modeled after Podkletnov's. They failed. Experts are skeptical that the device ever really worked in the first place. And since no one since then has been able to replicate the experiment—or build another device that combats the force of gravity—they're probably right. A few scientists say we just have to wait for the future. But many others think an antigravity machine is just plain impossible.

[AFTERWORD]

►A FUTURE PERSPECTIVE

IN THIS BOOK, you've learned about all sorts of things that haven't happened yet, and things that don't quite exist. How can we begin to guess at what the future holds? That's where experts called futurists come in.

When some people first hear the word "futurist," their imaginations run wild. They picture a fortune-teller with a crystal ball, a mystical figure who receives visions from a distant tomorrow. But in reality, any serious futurist will tell you—we don't make predictions, we make connections. That means that a futurist looks for present-day signals—observations, articles, research, data, tech trends—and finds connections among that information to imagine a set of possible scenarios that might arise in the coming years. In other words, the work of a futurist is connect-the-dots, not fill-in-the-blank. Some of these future scenarios may come true, and some may not. Either way, you'll always have a clearer perspective if you can think of the future—5, 10, even 15 years from now—as being a direct result of the conditions we see around us today.

The author of this book has done just that, sharing evidence of fascinating emerging technologies and new cultural trends and letting that evidence guide stories about our futures. Now you may be asking yourself—Why? Why spend time taking educated guesses about what the future holds when there's no way to know if you're right until we all see what happens? Whether you're a CEO developing your organization's long-term strategy, or a young person thinking about the next chapter of your life, the value of futurism is simple: It helps you prepare. The sooner you get a sense of where you and the people around you are headed, the sooner you can make plans to make the most of the world of tomorrow—and maybe even make it a better place in the process.

Marc Palatucci, Futurist

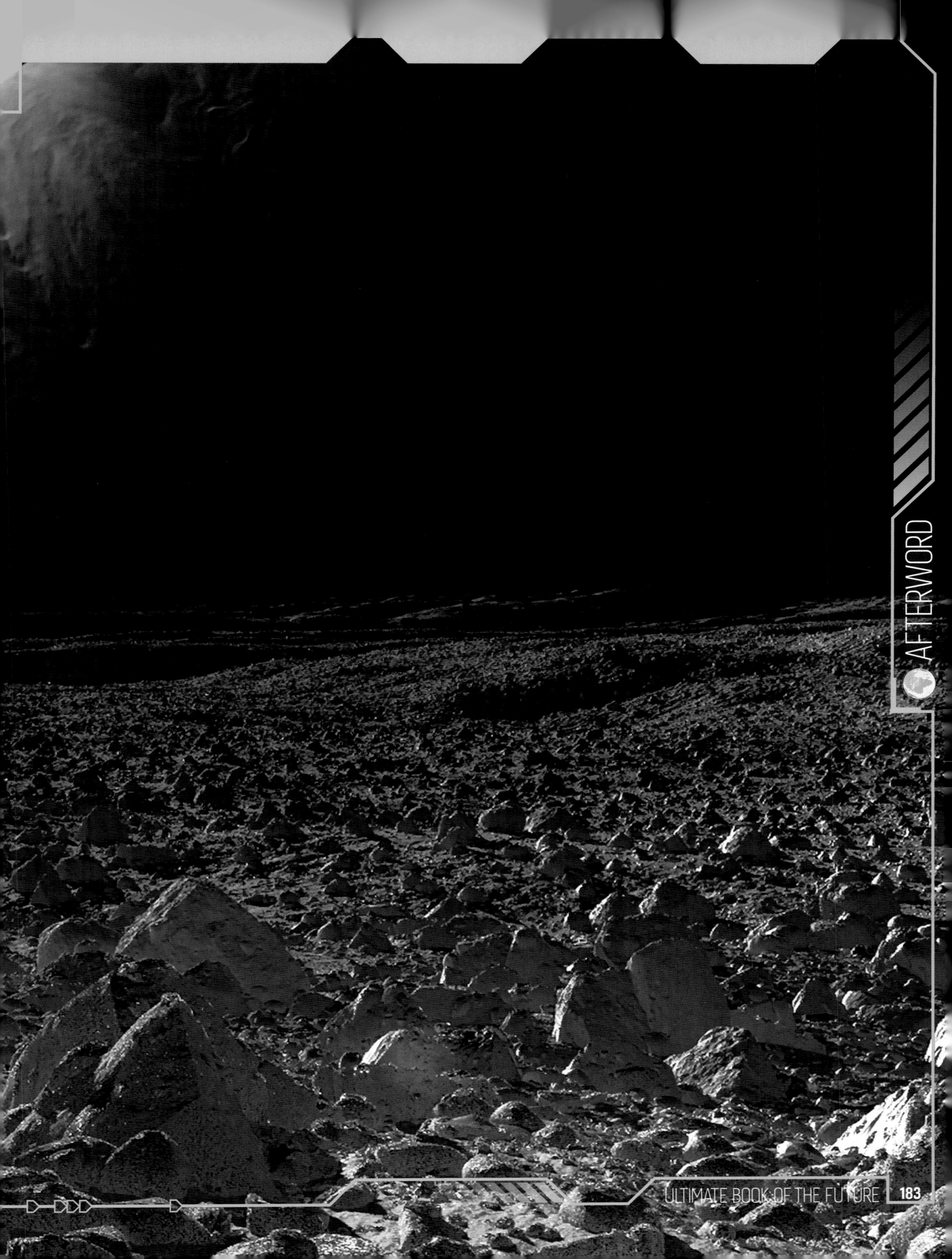

INDEX

INDEX
CONTINUED

CREDITS

Cover, Mondolithic Studios; back cover (LE), Tombot, Inc.; (UP RT), Ira Berger/Alamy Stock Photo; (LO RT), PERO studio/Shutterstock; 1 (CTR), Mondolithic Studios; 1 (throughout), ChalidMGM/Shutterstock; 4-5 (throughout), Dr Manager/Shutterstock; 4-5 (throughout), greenbutterfly/Shutterstock; 4 (UP), Daisy Daisy/Adobe Stock; 4 (LO LE), KevinHyde/Getty Images; 4 (CTR), NASA; 4 (LO RT), MINIWIZ Co., Ltd.; 5 (UP RT), PERO studio/Shutterstock; 5 (UP LE), Pierluigi Palazzi/Alamy Stock Photo; 5 (CTR), David/Adobe Stock; 5 (LO RT), Lexus/Sipa/Shutterstock; 6-7, Roman Budnyi/Alamy Stock Photo; **CHAPTER 1:** 8, Daisy Daisy/Adobe Stock; 10 (RT), John Phillips/Getty Images; 10-11, Ferrari/ZUMA Press/Newscom; 11, Keith Hamshere/Lucasfilm/20th Century Fox/Kobal/Shutterstock; 12-13, Mondolithic Studios; 14, Norman Chan/Dreamstime; 15 (LE), Sarcos Technology and Robotics Corporation; 15 (UP RT), Richard Williams/Mirrorpix/Newscom; 15 (LO RT), Elijah Nouvelage/Health-Exoskeleton/Reuters; 16 (LE), feelSpace; 16 (RT), Elizabeth Wald; 17 (LE), Future Grind, LLC; 17 (mouse), Tsekhmister/Shutterstock; 17 (LO RT), David J. Green-technology/Alamy Stock Photo; 18 (crickets), Melinda Fawver/Shutterstock; 18 (muffin), Charoen Krung Photography/Shutterstock; 18 (grasshopper), PetrP/Shutterstock; 19 (bowl and worms), Arco/J. Pfeiffer/Imagebroker/Alamy Stock Photo; 19 (termite on spoon), jassada watt/Adobe Stock; 19 (spoon with worms), Wittayayut/Getty Images; 19 (crab), Jan-Niklas Keltsch/Shutterstock; 20, The Washington Post/Getty Images; 20-21 (throughout), WhiteBarbie/Shutterstock; 20-21 (throughout), argus/Shutterstock; 20-21 (robot), phonlamaiphoto/Adobe Stock; 22 (LE), Walter Eric Sy/Shutterstock; 22 (RT), Shutterstock; 22-23 (fruit-filled pills), Shawn Hempel/Shutterstock; 22-23 (white pills and tablets), gomolach/Adobe Stock; 23 (hands

with cutlery), Prostock-studio/Shutterstock; 23 (plate with pill), kirill_makarov/Shutterstock; 24 (BOTH), Quirky China/Shutterstock; 25, Quirky China/Shutterstock; 26 (RT), Tombot, Inc.; 26 (LE), Jo Yong-Hak (South Korea Sci Tech Animals Society)/Reuters; 27 (UP), Splash/PetChatz/Newscom; 27 (LE), MR1805/iStock; 27 (LO), Dr. Alper Bozkurt; 28, Eloy Alonso/Reuters; 28-29, Framesira/Shutterstock; 29, Ira Berger/Alamy Stock Photo; 30 (LE), Dronathan Davis/Adobe Stock; 30 (Fail stamp, throughout), roland-topor/Shutterstock; 30 (RT), IFTN/Newscom; 30-31, Yakobchuk Olena/Adobe Stock; **CHAPTER 2:** 32, KevinHyde/Getty Images; 34-35, Splash News/Breitling/Newscom; 35 (UP), Unimedia/Shutterstock; 35 (LO), JetPack Aviation/MEGA/DCMIA/Newscom; 36-37, Mondolithic Studios; 38, Library of Congress, Prints and Photographs Division [LC-DIG-ggbain-28853]; 38-39 (LO), Rick Leisenring/Glenn H. Curtiss Aviation Museum; 38-39 (UP), EyePress/Newscom; 39, Cover Images/Newscom; 40, The Asahi Shimbun/Getty Images; 40-41, andrey_l/Shutterstock; 41, Steve Marcus/Reuters; 42, Paramount/AA Film Archive/Alamy Stock Photo; 42-43, local_doctor/Shutterstock; 43, Peter Jurik/Adobe Stock; 44, NASA/JPL/Space Science Institute; 45, Houston Mechatronics, Inc.; 46, mipan/Adobe Stock; 47, Dmitry Kalinovsky/Shutterstock; 48 (RT), Christophe Gateau/picture alliance/Getty Images; 48 (LO), Hermeus Corporation; 49 (UP), EM/MEGA/EMENC/Newscom; 49 (CTR), AP Photo/The Yomiuri Shimbun; 49 (LO), John Locher/AP/Shutterstock; 50-51, Limitless Space Institute; 50-51 (equations), EtiAmmos/Adobe Stock; 51, vchalup/Adobe Stock; **CHAPTER 3:** 52, NASA; 54-55, NASA; 55 (UP LE), George Ellswort/OurOwnsKIN; 55 (CTR), JSC/NASA; 55 (LO RT), NASA; 56 (UP), NASA; 56 (LO), NASA/JPL-Caltech; 57 (UP), ESA/Hubble, M. Kornmesser; 57 (LE),

Alan Dyer/VW PICS/Universal Images Group/Getty Images; 57 (LO), Gregoire Cirade/Science Source; 58, NASA/JPL-Caltech; 58-59, Mark Garlick/Science Source; 59, NASA/JPL-Caltech; 60-61, Victor Habbick Visions/Science Photo Library/Alamy Stock Photo; 61 (UP), Victor Habbick Visions/Science Source; 61 (LO), ustas/Adobe Stock; 62-63, Mondolithic Studios; 64-65, Geopix/Alamy Stock Photo; 65 (RT), NASA/JPL-Caltech; 65 (LO LE), NASA/JPL-Caltech/MSSS/JHU-APL; 66 (LE), JSC/NASA; 66 (RT), Hauke-Christian Dittrich/picture alliance/Getty Images; 67 (UP), JSC/NASA; 67 (LE), NASA's Ames Research Center/Dominic Hart; 67 (RT), NASA/JPL-Caltech; 68 (LO LE), NASA/JPL-Caltech/ULCA/JHU; 68-69 (asteroids), Paul Fleet/Dreamstime; 69, Esteban De Armas/Shutterstock; 70, Shutterstock; 71, Al Seib/Los Angeles Times/Getty; 72 (RT), Moviestore/Shutterstock; 72 (LO), Spencer Lowell/National Geographic Image Collection; 72-73, MasPix/Alamy Stock Photo; **CHAPTER 4:** 74, MINIWIZ Co.,Ltd.; 76, Mondolithic Studios; 78, Abaca Press/Alamy Stock Photo; 79 (UP), Lei Ting; 79 (CTR), Seabin Project/Bournemouth News/Shutterstock; 79 (LO), ekim/Adobe Stock; 80 (LE), Kees Veenenbos/National Geographic Image Collection; 80 (RT), Vladimir Melnikov/Adobe Stock; 81 (background), Beth J Harpaz/AP/Shutterstock; 81 (UP), Library and Congress, Prints and Photographs Division; 82 (LE), Dr. Mark R. Cutkosky; 82 (RT), Centauro; 83 (UP), Tom Libby, Kaushik Jayaram and Pauline Jennings. Courtesy of PolyPEDAL Lab UC Berkeley; 83 (CTR), Paul Marotta/Stringer/TechCrunch/Getty Images; 83 (LO), Platypus; 84-85, Jordan/Adobe Stock; 85, prasongtakham/Adobe Stock; 86, Billy H.C. Kwok/Bloomberg/Getty Images; 87 (UP RT), MINIWIZ Co. Ltd.; 87 (foreground), MINIWIZ Co., Ltd.; 88-89, Dr. Frederique Olivier; 89, Mark Carwardine/Nature

► FOR SLOANE. I CAN'T WAIT TO WATCH YOUR FUTURE UNFOLD. —SWD

Since 1888, the National Geographic Society has funded more than 14,000 research, conservation, education, and storytelling projects around the world. National Geographic Partners distributes a portion of the funds it receives from your purchase to National Geographic Society to support programs including the conservation of animals and their habitats. To learn more, visit natgeo.com/info.

For more information, visit nationalgeographic.com, call 1-877-873-6846, or write to the following address:

National Geographic Partners, LLC
1145 17th Street NW
Washington, DC 20036-4688 U.S.A.

For librarians and teachers: nationalgeographic.com/books/librarians-and-educators

More for kids from National Geographic: natgeokids.com

For rights or permissions inquiries, please contact National Geographic Books Subsidiary Rights: bookrights@natgeo.com

Designed by Brett Challos

Library of Congress Cataloging-in-Publication Data

Names: Drimmer, Stephanie Warren, author.
Title: Ultimate Book of the Future / Stephanie Warren Drimmer.
Description: Washington, D.C. : National Geographic Kids, 2022. | Audience: Ages 8-12 | Audience: Grades 4-6
Identifiers: LCCN 2019055275 | ISBN 9781426371622 (hardcover) | ISBN 9781426371639 (library binding)
Subjects: LCSH: Forecasting--Juvenile literature. | Technological forecasting--Juvenile literature.
Classification: LCC CB161 .D75 2021 | DDC 303.49--dc23
LC record available at https:/lccn.loc.gov/2019055275

The publisher would like the thank the book team: Kathryn Williams, project editor; Lori Epstein, photo director; Danny Meldung, photo editor; Chris Wren & Kenn Brown at Mondolithic Studios, illustrators; Joan Gossett, editorial production manager; Anne LeongSon and Gus Tello, design production assistants; Jen Geddes, fact-checker; and Marc Palatucci, expert reviewer.

Printed in China
22/PPS/1